John Mason Neale

Notes, Ecclesiological and Picturesque on Dalmatia, Croatia, Istria,

Styria

With a visit to Montenegro

John Mason Neale

Notes, Ecclesiological and Picturesque on Dalmatia, Croatia, Istria, Styria
With a visit to Montenegro

ISBN/EAN: 9783337244910

Printed in Europe, USA, Canada, Australia, Japan

Cover: Foto ©Andreas Hilbeck / pixelio.de

More available books at **www.hansebooks.com**

NOTES,

Ecclesiological and Picturesque,

ON

DALMATIA,
CROATIA, ISTRIA, STYRIA,

WITH

A VISIT TO MONTENEGRO.

BY THE

REV. J. M. NEALE, M.A.,

WARDEN OF SACKVILLE COLLEGE.

London:

J. T. HAYES, LYALL PLACE, EATON SQUARE.

1861.

PRINTED BY J. T. HAYES, LYALL-PLACE, EATON-SQUARE.

His Imperial Apostolic Majesty,

FRANCIS JOSEPH I.

THIS VOLUME

IS,

BY HIS MAJESTY'S GRACIOUS PERMISSION,

MOST RESPECTFULLY

DEDICATED.

CONTENTS.

CHAP.		PAGE.
I.	AUSTRIA PROPER, AND THE SALZKAMMERGUT	1
II.	STYRIA	16
III.	TRIESTE AND AQUILEIA	37
IV.	THE GLAGOLITA RITE	48
V.	ISTRIA	67
VI.	VEGLIA; OSSERO; AND TO ZARA	91
VII.	ZARA: SEBENICO	112
VIII.	SPALATO	135
IX.	MACARSKA, CURZOLA, CATTARO	156
X.	THE ECCLESIASTICAL DIVISIONS AND CHURCH POETRY OF DALMATIA	172
XI.	MONTENEGRO	182
XII.	RAGUSA; AND HOME	193

PREFACE.

The reasons which induced me to undertake the tour, an account of which the reader has before him, have been briefly detailed in the First Chapter.

I could not have carried it out with any advantage to the objects which I had in view, had it not been for the great kindness of His Excellency Count Apponyi, the Ambassador from Austria to this country. At the request of the Right Hon. W. E. Gladstone, to whom my warm thanks are also due, Count Apponyi favoured me with a very strong official recommendation to the authorities, both Ecclesiastical and Civil, in Dalmatia and the neighbouring provinces,—a document which proved most truly a golden key, opening every door, and surmounting every difficulty.

Notwithstanding the excellent works of Sir G. Wilkinson, Mr. Paton, and Mr. Adams, an ecclesiological account of Dalmatia had yet to be written. I may also add that, to the best of my knowledge, several parts of our tour—a portion of Istria, and the whole Island of Veglia, so curious from the Glagolita rite—have never yet been described by an English traveller.

Committee of the Ecclesiological Society), to have thrown any light on the churches (I have described exactly a hundred) of the seldom-visited countries of which my little volume treats.

And, with respect to the remarks in the former part of this Preface, it does seem that, at last, the wholesale confiscation of ecclesiastical property, and the butcherly cruelties perpetrated on Calabrian Royalists, are beginning to open men's eyes to the true character of the Italian Revolution.

If I may end with a reference to that class to whom these pages are principally addressed—what ecclesiologist (to take no higher view than that of a *mere* ecclesiologist) can fail to execrate the Government that has suppressed that most glorious Convent of Assisi, and left it the victim of complete and certain ruin?

SACKVILLE COLLEGE,
EAST GRINSTED, *June 6th*, 1861.

It is remarkable that the date of the above protest against Sacrilege should have been also that of its fearful Nemesis in the death of Count Cavour.

A TOUR IN DALMATIA.

Chapter I.

AUSTRIA PROPER, AND THE SALZKAMMERGUT.

I HAD long been desirous, as deeply interested in, and engaged on the history of, the Oriental Church, of observing for myself the mutual action and re-action of the Eastern and Western Communions in their border lands on the east coast of the Adriatic. As devoted to liturgical studies, I wished personally to examine, in the only country where it is still in use, the questions which arise from the venerable and mysterious Glagolita rite. And finally, as an ardent student of Ecclesiology, I promised myself no small gratification from the churches of Istria and Dalmatia,—and, above all, of Aquileia. At length, in the spring of last year, the opportunity, for which I had longed, presented itself.

I was happy enough to secure the companionship of my friend, the Rev. JOSEPH OLDKNOW, D.D., Perpetual Curate of Holy Trinity Chapel, Bordesley, whose many qualifications as a fellow traveller I had long since learnt, in the somewhat arduous tour in

Portugal, of which he has published an interesting little account. A community of interest in our pursuits and inquiries, and the perpetual cheerfulness and unvarying good humour of my companion,— would have been enough to make me forget inconveniences of a far graver character than any which it was our lot actually to encounter.

WE LEFT London on Tuesday, April 17, 1860, by way of Dover and Calais, for Paris. Proceeding by the Great Eastern of France, we devoted some days to the ecclesiology of Toul, Metz, and Strasburg. Hence, through snowstorms and bitter east wind, we made our way, by Karlsruhe and Bruchsal, to Stuttgart. Here we were most kindly received by His Excellency C. T. R. Gordon, Ambassador at the Court of Würtemburg, and one of the first ecclesiologists of our day; to whom our thanks are due for a most pleasant evening in his hospitable house.

Continuing our route by Esslingen, Ulm, and Augsburg, to Donauwerth, we then descended the river, whence that place derives its name, to Ratisbon. After giving two delightful days to that noble city, we resolved, as I was desirous of obtaining some idea of the churches in the Valley of the Danube, to continue our course by land. Up to this point, the chief ecclesiastical buildings of Würtemburg and Bavaria have been so carefully described by English ecclesiologists, especially by my friend, Mr. Webb, in his admirable work, that I could not hope to add anything to the results of their researches. Ratisbon passed, I am treading ground not described, I believe,

—at least not described in print,—by my fellow students.

The Valley of the Danube, then, from Donauwerth to Passau, abounds in churches, for the most part, framed in the same mould. Generally speaking, small, they have chancel or nave with north or south aisle; tower, anywhere rather than at the west end; tallish, the square surmounted by, not bevelled into, an octagon: and that finished by a (later) bulb and spirelet. The square, preponderates over the apsidal, east end; and the further we advance east, the more completely is this the case. Who will solve for us this great problem?—Why is England the mother country of the one, France of the other, school? and why do stone vaultings and gabled towers belong to the latter, wooden roofs and square towers, or spires, to the former? This, I take it, is one of the deepest questions in ecclesiology.

As might be expected in a land so often ravaged by war, there is comparatively—to all appearance—little of ancient work. The peculiar taste of the Jesuits, too, once so powerful in Bavaria, shows itself in the heavy gilding, stuccoed domes, and painted vaultings,—(frequently representing the history of the Patron Saint)—everywhere to be seen. The larger churches seem to have had a series of narrow chapels, with elaborate vaulting, external to the nave aisles: this is to be seen, for example, in the parish church of Wilshofen, our first day's journey from Ratisbon. The road from this place to Passau runs close to the Danube all the way, and is seldom far from the railway. I

Wilshofen.

saw these two churches between Wilshofen and Passau:

Hasbruch. *Hasbruch* is a very curious building, the railway (then in progress, since opened) touches the churchyard wall. Circular externally, it is octagonal within,—without constructional choir, porch, or original tower; though, with execrable taste, the latter was added in 1762. The original pitch of the pyramid-like roof, which is very ancient, is preserved, and has a fine and very singular effect. There is a central pier, as in a Chapter-house—circular, with octagonal

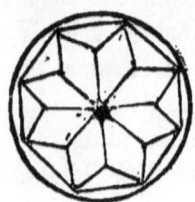

base and the ribs spring immediately from the upper part without any capital. The vaulting is thus:— On three of the cardinal sides, there is an ugly broad lancet; there is also a western door; the whole is evidently of Flamboyant work. I should like to know whether the peculiar shape of this church is a mere freak of the architect,—or whether a specimen of a local type. There is another entrance by a gallery and circular turret, from—what is now—a farm on the south side, but which I suppose to have been a religious house; not the least curious part of the whole arrangement.

Santpor. Next we came to *Santpor*, a small Flamboyant church. Chancel,—nave,—south tower, apse trigonal; windows of two lights, trefoiled with awkward quatrefoil in lead. Nave,—of two bays, with an ugly lancet on each side. The checkie vaulting of the chancel and nave, evidently later, is very singular. The tower is nearly square, with pyramidal heading.

The road continues between the future railway and the river, till the towers of Passau come in sight. This, episcopal city though it be, has but little to interest an ecclesiologist. The situation is unspeakably grand; the Danube, with the bold heights beyond; the larger Inn, obedient in its course, and henceforth to take its name from its inferior rival; and the black Ilz pouring into the united streams from the opposite side, at the moment of their junction. Here I would recommend an inn not mentioned by the guide-books, the *Grünen Engel;* where we were very comfortably off. All the churches are modern, though here and there with traces of old work. *S. Michael* has nothing interesting; I here heard the devotion of the Stations—it was a Friday —gone through with considerable earnestness by a large congregation. Beyond this, is the once conventual church of *S. Paul*, a huge Italian building, with stucco, gilding, and painting, to the heart's delight of the seventeenth century. On the north side are some poor remains of early Flamboyant cloisters, and a square-headed entrance-door, very good, of that date. Among the earlier mural monuments of this cloister, several are to the Abbesses. Beyond this again, the *Jesuits' Church*, really worthless. Going down the Danube—it was a day of continuous rain— I found a church of which I could not learn the name; only so far curious, that, amidst all the tinsel work of the seventeenth century, it has evident remains of a Romanesque narthex, the arches singularly stilted. The *Cathedral* stands on a height; the nave was rebuilt, after having

Passau,
S. Michael.

S. Paul.

Jesuits' Church.

Cathedral.

been destroyed by fire, in 1665; the choir, though too much mutilated to be worth a description, must have been very fine Flamboyant, (1407—1450). Beyond the Inn is the church of *S. Gertrude* entirely modern.

S. Gertrude.

The chief devotion here is that of *Maria Hilf*, whose church, behind the Inn-Stadt, with the black wonder-working image of Our Lady, is a celebrated pilgrimage. It is reached by an ascent of 264 steps, up which you may see many a devout pilgrim toiling on his knees, and repeating a Pater Noster or Ave at each. Every little print shop has its view of Passau shadowed by the guardian care of Our Lady of Good Help.

The scenery of the Danube from Passau to Linz is very fine; though the rain still continued, the contrast was striking, as we saw it, between the sombre tint of the fir-clad mountains, that rise on either side, and the vivid young green of the spring chesnuts scattered here and there among them. Patches of snow at this, the end of April, still lay heavy on the upper hills, and drifts and tails of cloud dragged themselves here and there over the rocky heights. So down the river, dark, turbid, and swollen,—with half an hour's stoppage at Engelhardtzell, the Austrian frontier,— to Linz. We were at the *Rother Krebs*, which is on the left bank of the river, and close to the water's edge; very comfortable quarters. The view from the window of our vaulted room, which commanded that part of Linz which lies on the other side of the Danube, rather reminded me—to compare small things with great—of that which you have of Cologne from the Belle Vue at Deutz.

Linz, though the capital of Upper Austria, is a very dull place for an ecclesiologist. We were there on the second Sunday after Easter. First to the *Cathedral*, a modern and utterly worthless building. There was a good congregation, and a very fair sermon on the orphanhood of the Disciples during the ten days of our LORD's departure. Then to *All Angels*, also a modern church, where we heard a very good military mass. I was much struck, in the offertory, with the soft and gentle strains in which the—*A woman when she is in travail hath sorrow*, was given, compared with the jubilant expression of thankfulness in—" She remembereth no more her anguish for joy,—*for joy*,—FOR JOY,—that a man is born into the world;" so completely carrying out the mediæval interpretation of the long travail of the Church; and then to thankfulness that, at the end of four thousand years,—The Man, the long-promised God Man, should be born into the world.

_{Linz Cathedral.}

In the great square, on the northern side of the river, is a most profane juxtaposition of three pillars, —the Trinity Column in the centre, surmounted with the most offensive type of seventeenth century productions, and raised in consequence of the deliverance of Linz from cholera,—on one side a column bearing a statue of Neptune, on the other, a pillar surmounted with Jupiter. Crossing the long wooden bridge, 1700 feet in length, we visited a church in the southern quarter, as worthless as the others. I could obtain no information regarding the magnificent Gothic Cathedral about to be erected here.

In the afternoon, the railway, running through a very dull country, takes us to Lambach. We reach that place about four—and now the Salzkammergut mountains, among which we are so soon going to plunge, stand out clear and blue to S. and S.W. As we enter the quaint little town, we pass the great Benedictine House, still in full work, and take up our abode at a quiet little country inn, the *Schwarzes Rössel*. And first, again passing the monastery, and descending a steep hill, we make our way along the side of the green Traun to the bluff hill of *Baura*, round which the village niches itself in various green nooks. A pleasant field walk, with cowslips, ox-eyes, orchises, and forget-me-nots, to tell how forward, after our late mountain passes, spring was here in the lowlands, I may quote what follows from a letter written the same night— " First through a lovely valley, starred with cowslips, to the church of Baura. This stands on a high bit of table land, that almost overhangs the town; a most pleasant situation; the green river foaming beneath; wooded banks on its other side. Look up the stream, and the Benedictine Monastery crowns the opposite height; look south, and you have the chain of purple mountains, snow-striped and speckled, great Traunstein towering above the rest. Baura is dedicated to the Blessed Trinity, and was built in 1755. It is triangular; has three doors, three windows, three sacristies, three organs, and is built of three sorts of Sicilian marble, and cost 333,333 florins. Over the first entrance I read, *Deum Patrem Creatorem Mundi, venite adoremus;* opposite in a wretched transparency

[marginal note: Baura, H. Trinity.]

behind the altar, is a very offensive picture of the FATHER. Over the second door, *Deum Filium Redemptorem Mundi, venite adoremus ;* and opposite, our LORD's Ascent from the Cross. Over the third, *Deum Sanctum Spiritum, venite adoremus ;* and opposite, the Nativity; I suppose, as brought to pass by the operation of the HOLY GHOST.

" From Baura we walked back to the monastery at Lambach : it consists of two or three quadrangles, with lines of whitewashed square-headed windows, some two hundred years old. But the foundation is of the eleventh century ; and there it is in life. We were shown into the church by a servant ; there is nothing whatever in it. I ask for the library ; it is not to be seen. I send in my recommendation; out comes the Librarian, one of the Fathers, a very pleasing man, rather tall and stout, about fifty. He took us over it; it has 14,000 volumes ; manuscripts of great value, and an almost priceless collection of ecclesiastical Incunabula. *What are Incunabula?* you ask. It is the name that Germans give to books printed before 1500. I found some pretty little manuscript breviaries : but manuscript missals there were none. At last I got two early printed ones, Augsburg and Frisingen ; and finding some sequences not yet reprinted, asked if I might have them to copy at the inn. This could not be done unless application was made to the ' Prelate.' They had just finished supper: it was nearly seven : we were shown into the little refectory. The Abbat was a very striking man, I imagine about forty, by far the most intellectual looking of the whole set; only to be distinguished from the rest by a gold pectoral cross.

'Certainly we should have the books; was there anything else he could do for us?' 'Might we attend compline and matins?' 'What were we?' 'Priests of the English Church.' 'Surely, why not?' Then he sent for some wine of the monastery's own growth, and we and the fathers had each a tumbler. Before we had finished, the bell for compline rang. The little hours were said, not in the church, but in a small oratory. At its east end is no altar, but a cross. The stalls, which have misereres, are not returned, and there is a kind of ante-chapel. The Abbat sat in the westernmost stall of the north side, and gave me, as the post of honour, the place on his left hand. Opposite to him was the prior. Service began by a German lection, a translation of S. Bernard, by the Prior. In about ten minutes, the Abbat rang a little bell, and the reader stopped. Then began the ordinary compline service. That ended, except the last benediction, a Probationer read in German, a prayer, asking forgiveness for that day's sins, and a resolution to sin no more. This resolution was repeated by the fathers in common. Then the Abbat, also in German, said, 'Remember that, as you are now about to lie down in your beds, so some day shall you lie down in your graves. Remember that, as you for yourselves close your eyes in sleep, so some day they must be closed for you in death. Remember that, as you cover yourselves with your bed-clothes, so some day you will be wrapped in the shroud.' Then he gave the benediction, sprinkled the others with holy water, but gave it us to take for ourselves. The service, I ought to say, was on the monotone, except the hymn and the antiphon and

Nunc Dimittis, but very striking from the depth of voices. There are about five and twenty fathers and brethren. Back to the inn; coffee: then I sat up late writing out the sequences. At 3·30, very unwillingly, I confess, up again; and I was soon knocking at the gate of the Quadrangle. I had my old place by the Abbat. Matins began at 4·0, were over about 5·10; they were simply Benedictine, without any local peculiarity: Psalms said on the monotone, antiphons, &c., sung. And then I went to bed for three hours more, with sufficient satisfaction."

There is a railway from Lambach to Gmunden, on the Traunsee, but we preferred engaging a kind of car; and accordingly early the next morning we were passing the Benedictine Monastery; and crossing the Traun, Baura long towering to our right, we made our way south. Our first church was *Roitham*. It has chancel, nave, south porch, and western tower. The whole is of Flamboyant date. Trigonal apse: choir of two bays and a-half; nave of three; vaulting very elaborate. There is one of those strange original western galleries which we shall find accompanying us even as far as Croatia; and which, for want of a better term, I shall name narthex-galleries. They are of stone; always Flamboyant; sometimes stretched from aisle-wall to aisle-wall; sometimes from pier to pier; have one, or two, or three bays, from east to west. The present example has four bays, from north to south; one from east to west, with eight-clustered shafts, and very singular and elaborate vaulting. The use of these erections I cannot even guess. Were they for the choir—which would agree with its posi-

Roitham.

tion in Portuguese churches—or for some particular class of worshippers—as women? The font is rather small, dodecagonal (this we shall find a local peculiarity): sides slightly concave, circular base. The internal door of the south porch is a square-headed trefoil, with rich inter-penetrating mouldings; the vaulting, thus, very rude:

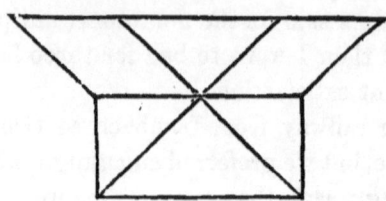

There is an external benatura, as always here. The tower is thin and tall, of six stages, divided by strings, but without windows. Under an open lean-to on the south side of the nave, is a representation of The Agony. I venture to quote from another letter.

"Here we left our vehicle, and scrambled down hill to the Traunsfall. It is partly spoilt by the river having been, to a certain degree, canalised for a mill; but still a very grand sight. The deep green of the water; a kind of purple haze on the outside of the spray; the thunder of the fall, pent in, and echoed by the steep banks. The fall somewhat resembles a capital E: the mill stands at the lower end, and from one of the outhouses, which actually overhangs the stream, is the best view. I suppose the height to be 30 feet; the breadth of the river, 80 yards; depth of water, 7 or 8 feet. Hence, it is by far the most magnificent cascade I ever saw, and it gave one such great quiet peaceful thoughts; made one (I know not why) think more of God's love than His power. I leant over the thunder of the water for some twenty minutes; the spray-rainbow sometimes arching above my head; and thought how utterly untrue those lines of Byron's are about—

> The hell of waters! where they howl and hiss,
> And boil in endless torture: where the sweat
> Of their great agony is wrung from this
> Their Phlegethon,—

and how much more naturally one's thoughts dwell on the "voice of many waters round the throne," of which this, the 'Alleluiatic Sequence' of the earthly river is the faint type. On again: to *Laakir-* Laakirchen. *chen.* Here the schoolmaster brought in a school to say their mid-day prayers in church "They may kiss your hand, may they not?" said he. So the little mites, 40 or 45 in number, had that honour, and passed on, as I made the sign of the cross over each, with great content. Pretty children they were too. You know the beauty of the girls and women in this part of Austria is proverbial."

This church is a very singular building, of Flamboyant date, with south sacristy, chancel, nave, narthex-gallery, western tower, south porch. The hexagonal apse, and chancel of two bays, are modernised. The nave is most remarkable: it has two bays for itself, two for the gallery. In the *centre* of the former half is a pier; circular stilted base, voluted stem, then becoming four-partite: no cap. The vaulting suits this arrangement. The gallery has, north to south, four bays, east to west two; the mouldings very elaborate.

The piers are octagonal, with concave sides. There was an original stone staircase of sixteen steps on the south side. The font is small; the south porch almost a fac-simile of that at Roitham. The western tower has that remarkable singularity, a south door. It has five stages, separated by strings; only one little square-beaded light in the uppermost; it is double-gabled. On the west end is this date, I₈Vl, which I read 1446. The external appearance of the whole building is very picturesque, from the enormous pitch of both choir and nave, and the great length of roof where the lean-to joins the former.

The country now rapidly increases in sublimity; we pass the brow of the hill, and the Traunsee, like a gem set in a shrine of purple mountains, breaks on us; *Gmunden* couching picturesquely on the near side. We alight at the inn,—the *Sonne*. Mine host proffers *forelle* and kid: we order them, and go to the church,

Gmunden. a building of some pretensions. Chancel, nave, two aisles to the latter, narthex-gallery, western tower, north and south porches; the whole Flamboyant. All the windows are modernised. The apse is hexagonal; choir of one bay, vaulted separately; the nave of three. The piers are very poor and awkward, circular on square base; no caps. The gallery extends only across the nave; three bays north to south, one east to west. The tower is engaged; the aisles are awkwardly carried along it with a half arch. In the north* aisle, north of the tower, is a very fine altar, in its way, of red marble, the reredos of

* So it is in my notes; but my memory strongly suggests the *south*.

the same material, with the souls in purgatory below; a landscape resembling the valley of the Traun above: all this is in white marble and high relief. There is this chronogram :—

paVCa Ceres æsus speCIesqVe MerI CererIsVe
sIC hIC fLagrantes Igne pIante pIat.

i.e. 1653. This church is the first in which we have seen any preparations for the month of Mary, and they are very slight here. The north and south porches resemble those at Roitham. Near the south is a rudely executed figure of a knight in bas-relief, with the date, 1497. Dinner over, we go on board the steamer which takes us to the southern extremity of the lake.

Oh that lake! how marvellously beautiful it is! The passage took seventy-five minutes; and an intelligent passenger told me the names of each mountain, as to our left—for, on the right, the scenery is more pastoral —it peered over the blue waters. Traunstein rises, monarch of all before us; but, in succession, fir-capped Erloch-kufel, purple Hundstein, wild Hirschen-belt, double-peaked Schnee-marl, lordly Radelstein, precipitous Spitzel, and uttermost Dartstein. And so we land in the quaint little town of Ebensee.

We send our luggage on in a car; ourselves walking up the valley of the Traun, ten miles, to Ischl.

Can I ever forget—can I, or any one else, ever describe — the glorious scenery of that mountain walk?

Chapter II.

STYRIA.

We were said to be the first visitors at Ischl; and whatever the Hotel Kaiserinn Elizabeth may be in the season, it seemed to us a cold, desolate, rambling, barn-like place now. Glad enough we were to have the stove of our great room lighted; and then they served us a sufficiently good dinner. Next morning, with some difficulty, we changed a ten-pound note, and therewith procured an *einspänniger Wagen*, which we resolved never to do again: its pace being not three miles an hour. *Lauffen* was our Lauffen, first church, and a sufficiently curious one; chancel, nave, south chapel to the former, and south aisle to the latter; western tower. The chancel is modernised and painted: apse pentagonal. The south chapel has also a projecting pentagonal apse, with a well-defined apse arch. The nave has three bays; the piers are circular on octagonal base, and without caps; the responds singularly bold and good. The font is dodecagonal, on circular base, and that on square plinth. The internal door of the tower has an excellent iron grill; for we are now on the borders of Styria; and I have no doubt that we shall find King David's rule, "Iron for things of iron," carried out to the full. The tower itself is modern. In the church-yard there is an ossuary, such as I have seen in Bretagne, the sculls arrayed on shelves; with a Maltese cross, and the name, inscribed on each forehead. A glorious mountain towers to the south immediately above the church. From here our route continues through a magnificent valley, with occasional patches of snow on the higher peaks; but already Pötschl begins to lift himself up in front, towering more precipitously every hundred yards that we advance. At seven miles from Ischl, we reach *Goisling*. This is a Protestant village; traditionally so, far beyond the time of Luther, and connected, I suppose, with the Turlupins of the middle ages. The people are now, however, red-hot Lutherans; and my companion, peeping through the windows of their place of worship, reported that the altar was decked out with candlesticks and crucifix, after the ordinary Lutheran fashion. The village church, nevertheless, which serves the minority of the inhabitants, is Catholic. It is not at all easy to understand, and has been very much modernised. I take it that, being originally a cross church, the south transept has been turned into the choir; the original chancel contains some fair Flamboyant work; the tower at the west-end is tall, thin, and modernised. The font here, also, is dodecagonal, and clearly by the same hand as that at Lauffen. Still proceeding eastward, we come to the fork of the road, whereof the right branch goes to Hallstadt and the left to Aussee; and in a few minutes more stop at a church, which the villagers called Stagga, and which, with some little trouble, I make out to be *S. Agatha*. It has chancel, nave, and western tower; the apse is tri-

Goisling.

S. Agatha.

c

gonal; the choir has two bays, with elaborate late vaulting. The nave is spoilt with a flat roof of 1853. The windows of the nave are, I think, Middle-pointed, of two lights, trefoiled, quatrefoil in head; the exterior arch, ogee. The south door is round-headed Flamboyant. The east-end is blocked up by a huge painting of the Passion; the rock of the Sepulchre is represented on each side of the altar. The font, also dodecagonal, is by the same hand as the two last, though rather inferior. This village is full of enormous piles of pine wood; for one of the great mountain slides passes close to it; and all the time that I was taking the church, I could hear the occasional avalanches of pines, leaping and crashing down their troughs. There was also a may-pole outside the church. And now we began to ascend Pötschl, taking another horse at S. Agatha. The ascent is made with but few zigzags; the enormous squadrons of forest-trees that cluster the mountain almost to the top, are very striking. Up at that height, the height of Snowdon, it was a pleasant spring day; the primroses and violets peeped out where the snow had melted; and the sun, which had considerable power, brought forth all the fragrance of the young turpentine, not less sweet, I thought, than the incense which the gum-cistus of Portuguese mountains sends up at morning and evening to heaven.

Here I had a long talk with a poor wood-cutter who was going to Aussee, and whose basket of tools we slung on behind our carriage. He told me, that two springs ago he had lost his only son, Franz, in one of the timber-slides. He and the boy were just about to

sit down to their dinner by the side of one higher up
the mountain, when a hungry dog made a snatch at
the cloth in which it was folded up, crossed the slide,
and was carrying it off. The boy jumped up and ran
after him; but his foot slipped in the slide, in which
some snow was lying, and before he could extricate
himself, a huge pine came down and dashed him to
pieces. "And between twelve and one," said the
father, "which was too wicked," because it is understood that no timber is felled or sent down at the
dinner hour. The pine forests do not reach quite to
the top of the mountain; and on a bare piece of
common land, bleak and desolate, stands a stone which
divides the Styrian from the Austrian Salzkammergut.
A long, but easy and well-engineered descent, brings
us into Aussee, the capital of the latter district. Here
we had the happy intelligence at the inn that there
were firstrate *forelle*; so having ordered them to be
boiled blue, as the phrase goes, we went out to see the
churches. The parish church is of very
considerable size; it has chancel, nave,   Aussee.
south aisle to each, south chapel with crypt, and
north chapel. The apse is pentagonal, but modernised; in its north-west bay there is a sacrament-house
which reaches to the top of the constructional arch;
it is very late, almost Italian. The choir has one
bay with very elaborate vaulting: the nave three;
there are great pews with doors. Here again we
found a narthex gallery. The tower at the west
end is very lofty; of five stages, divided curiously
enough, by strings, or rather sets-off, of shingle;
there you see the effects of the pine forests, for this

shingle is of deal: it has a gabled pyramidal head. The south door is Flamboyant, with an original image of S. Peter; and to your right, as you enter, is the south chapel of which I have spoken, and the crypt, both modernised.

In returning from this church, my companion having gone to look after the *forelle*, I hit on a curious chapel which was the cause of their being completely spoilt. It is very small, with pentagonal apse, nave of two bays and narthex gallery; the windows in its apse, five lancets; the whole building appears Firstpointed. But its interest is concentrated in a magnificent triptych. When open it is thus :—

2	3
1	4

Maria Memento Mei.
1889.

In the centre is the usual fifteenth-century representation of the Blessed TRINITY, the FATHER seated holding the Crucifix, while the HOLY GHOST hovers between the two figures. Six saints, but not marked with any especial attribute, stand on each side. The leaves, when open, are thus :—

1. Eight saints, unmarked with any especial attri-

bute: above them a legend which I could not decypher.
2. A Pope, a Cardinal, a Bishop, and other Saints.
3. An Emperor and Empress.
4. Several saints, all of them in the religious habit.
This closed, the arrangement is as follows:—

1	2	3	4	5	6
7	8	9	10	11	12
		13			

1. S. Katherine. 2. S. Barbara. 3. The Annunciation. 4. The Visitation. 5. S. Dorothea. 6. S. Margaret. 7. S. Lucy. 8. S. Apollonia. 9. The Nativity. 10. The Epiphany. 11. S. Agnes. 12. Female Saint, (? who). 13. S. Veronica, with an angel at each end of the compartments holding at the handkerchief. Under all: A. E. I. O. U., the well-known Austrian device, Austriæ Est Imperare Orbi Universo. The whole is extremely well painted.

On the south side is another triptych. When open, thus:

1	2	3

1 and 3 are occupied by the apostles. In 1 S. Bartholomew, S. Matthew, S. James, S. Simon, S. Peter (with one key, vested entirely in white), S. Philip.

In 3 S. Philip (repeated), S. John, S. Matthew, S. Andrew, S. Judas, S. James the Less.

At the back of 1 is The Agony in the Garden.

At the back of 3 are S. Sebastian, S. Roche, S. Wolfgang (a bishop with a church in his hands).

In 2. S. Eustachius, with the hart (I give the names as here spelled).

S. Panthaleon, in a red cloak.

S. Jeorg, with the Dragon.

S. Achatius, only head to be seen in red cap, and hand holding a hart's horn.

S. Veyt [Vitus], holding a cup with flame in it.

S. Dyonisius, holding a *second* head in his hands.

S. Erasmus, with his bowels wound round a roller.

S. Nycla, with book and three golden bells.

S. Gyles, with his stag.

S. Lambert, with chains.

S. Margaret, a very sweet face; the little dragon peeps out from behind S. Christopher.

S. Christopher, leaning on tree; our LORD as a naked child standing upright, a red cruciferous nimbus.

S. Katherine, with sword, but no wheel.

S. Barbara, with tower and chalice.

These triptychs are as interesting as any that I have ever seen. They are in very good preservation, and ought surely to be well copied while in so perfect a state. The chapel has a little octagonal spirelet.

After dinner we continue our course along the same valley, to the not very interesting church of *Mitterndorff*, entirely Flamboyant. It has chancel, nave, north transept, western tower. The apse is trigonal; its windows of three lights, trefoiled. Here again the vaulting is very elaborate. The nave has two bays; the narthex-gallery three from north to south, one from east to west. The tower is much modernised. *Mitterndorff.*

Evening gathered in. The great mountain Grimming raised himself higher and higher, the shepherd's call, the goat-bell, the mill-wheel died off into silence; and it was almost dark, when, forcing our way through the great pass, where rocks and hills were on this side and on that, we came out in the green valley of the Enns. It is too dark to notice the country,—we drop off to sleep, and rouse ourselves as the carriage draws up at Steinach.

I remember the Post there as a genuine mountain-inn with true Austrian kindness to make our fare,—eggs and fish, doubly pleasant. We are early on our way again; and the first church which we reach is *Lietzen*. Apse, nave, western tower, for there is no constructional chancel. The apse trigonal, the windows of two trefoiled lights with a trefoil in head. I am inclined to believe these, and consequently the church—notwithstanding a certain laxity of mouldings,—Middle pointed. All the other windows are gutted. The nave has three bays; the vaulting is very elaborate. There is a plain *Lietzen.*

western door, and a large ogee-arched benatura by its side.

Through the valley, now winding between less abrupt mountains, we reach *Rottenmann;* one of the churches which owes their foundation to the great iron forges belonging to the Monks of Admont. Apse, transept, nave, western tower, porch west of that. Apse, trigonal; central window, three lights; side lights unfoliated; central light trefoiled; north window, two plain lights; south as central, only an ogee transom bisects it. The whole seems Middle-pointed. The vaulting is here again rather elaborate. Windows in transepts, north and south, as central one in apse. There is a little south chapel in the nave, by the tower, with one lancet. The narthex-gallery has four bays, north and south; two east and west. The staircase has its original single light. The tower, of four stages, quite plain; belfry windows of two lights. The western porch has a parvise; its window, of three lights, has the central cinqfoiled. This is a quaint, rather than interesting church.

Rottenmann.

On by a good road, without much scenery, though at one part we reach an elevation of 5,000 feet. We take *Geishorn,* a very poor church. Chancel, nave, west tower. The chancel modernised; the nave of two bays; tower, four stages, with tiled stringcourses, then pyramidal headed. This day, considering the character of Austrian posting, we made a capital journey—sixty-one miles—and reached the picturesque town of Leoben about dusk. We slept at the Goldner Adler, in the great square,— a very fair inn.

Geishorn.

Next morning, crossing the Mur, to the church of *S. Maria am Wogen.* It has chancel, nave, north chapel to the former, and narthex-gallery. The whole is of Flamboyant date. The apse, pentagonal; the central window, blocked; the pair north and south of it of three, the next pair of two, trefoiled lights. There is some fair stained glass, principally from our blessed LORD's Life. The entrance to the north chapel is by a door of very good moulding, the arch very much depressed. The nave, of four bays; the fifth being taken up by the gallery. The first three had, originally, on each side a Flamboyant window of three trefoiled lights. The gallery, which slightly projects beyond its own bay, has two bays from east to west, three from north to south: the mouldings and piers are very excellent. The panelling in front of the upper part is remarkable,—an arcade of twelve trefoiled lights, and thoroughly "Perpendicular." You would take it for a bit of English panelling. This church, though without aisles, is larger than most, even town churches. It is beset with pews, mostly doored pews.

Outside there is a western lean-to narthex, almost past the furthest bounds which even courtesy can assign to Flamboyant. The tower, which is engaged, and at the west end of the nave, is modern. I observed here, about 10 a.m., a great number of people praying by the graves of their relatives. The churchyard wall is arcaded: a good deal of sculpture, from scriptural and other subjects, some of it coloured, is introduced.

Two other churches which we saw here, one the Franciscan, the other, on the hill, but of which I could not learn the dedication, are valueless.

We then hired a conveyance for the railway at Bruck. The road, running along the north bank of the Mur, is always pleasing, in some parts highly romantic; much of the beauty was lost to us by continuous wet weather. *Michelsdorff* was the only church we saw. This has chancel, nave, and engaged western tower. The chancel is only the trigonal apse; the windows are modernised. The nave has three bays, with elaborate vaulting, but the windows are entirely modern. There is no narthex gallery. I have no note of the tower.

<small>Michelsdorff.</small>

Now on to Bruck-an-der-Mur. I never remember more pouring weather. We only saw the church which lies nearest to the railway station, though on the other side of the Mur: this is the *Minorites'*. It has chancel, nave, north chapel, but, according to the frequent practice of that order, no tower. The apse is pentagonal. A great gutted lancet occupies each side; these might have been, and I rather fancy were, two-light Middle-pointed windows. The chancel, of two bays, is singularly excellent; in each bay on both sides, is a Middle-pointed window of two trefoiled lights—a circle in head; the mouldings very delicate. The vaulting is simply cross, the vaulting shafts and corbels are very pretty. The nave is utterly ruined by " restoration." There is a modern gallery, no doubt replacing the narthex gallery. The cloisters, on the south side, are also modernised.

<small>Bruck. The Minorites'.</small>

The railway to Gratz runs through the most glorious scenery,—so say the books,—but to us it was merely fog and rain. We did not see a hundred yards before us, till we found ourselves comfortably settled in the Elephant, a very fair inn, decorated with the figure of that animal, of life-like size, on the stable wall.

Gratz is like a little Vienna,—from the city itself being of confined dimensions, and separated from the suburbs by the fortifications, now planted, and places of public recreation. The former citadel, the centre of all, is near the Schlossberg, a steep hill on the north of the river, whence you enjoy a fine view of the whole neighbourhood. Commencing from the east, you see the Jakomini Vorstadt; casting your eye over the river, you have the Gries, the Cailan,— then south-east, the parish of S. Andrew,—then S. Elizabeth, S. George, the Maria Hilf,—which brings us to the south-west; again crossing the river, the Graben,—then, north-west, the high hill called the Rosenberg,—the suburbs of Unten-and Ober-Geydorf,—then north, the Morelerfeld—and so round by the Münzgraben to the Jakomini, whence we set out.

While we stand on this same Schlossberg, we may as well hear a little of the early history of Gratz, now a city of 65,000 inhabitants, and the capital of Styria. The first time the name occurs is in a deed of October 14, 881, in which King Louis changes with the Archbishop Dietman, certain lands at Maulstadt against certain others in Gratz. From that time onwards, we find it spelt Graetz, Grüz, Gretz, Grez, Gratz, or Graz. But since 1843, through the efforts of the learned native, Von Hammer Purgstall, the last-mentioned way has prevailed. In 1163, we find the place a town of some importance; but not till 1435 was it completely fortified. The Turk-storm burst over Styria in 1532, under Ibrahim Pacha, but Graz stood firm. In 1807, the French destroyed the citadel,—and thence came the hill where we stand. Lutheranism made a great but unsuccessful struggle for this place,—and at present, the Protestants, though they have a chapel, are a very inconsiderable body.

The Cathedral of S. Giles, Graz.
Now we go down to the *Cathedral.* It is placed well, on a height, just opposite the University. On the ground where it now stands, was built, in 1157, the S. Egidikirchlein; in 1450, Frederick IV, surnamed the Powerful, began the present erection,—and the main structure was finished in 1462. It now consists of chancel, nave with aisles, and north and south chapels; western tower. The centre length is 256 feet; breadth, 120; height (they say, but I can hardly credit it), 118. The apse is trigonal; each side has a Flamboyant window of three trefoiled lights. The high altar, of red flaked marble, has a tolerable painting of S. Giles, by Joseph Flurer, a scholar of Salvator Rosa. The stained glass in the eastern windows is execrable. On the north side is the Imperial Royal Chapel; a very elegant projecting stone gallery, rather frittered away, however, by over decoration; amidst much trash, there is a very interesting wall-painting of our LORD on the Cross, on a gold ground (1475) surrounded by

warriors and priests. The chancel has four and a half bays; the vaulting is more elaborate than beautiful. On the epistle side of the altar is a curious *ex voto* of one Peter de Poinds (+ at Graz, 1633), Chamberlain of Charles II, the crucifix surrounded by kneeling figures representing his master's children. The bodies of SS. Maxentius and Vincentius rest here, —on the opposite side, the relics of the Virgin Martyr Maxentia.

The nave has five bays,—the arches are decidedly poor. The piers themselves consist of four shafts, set on angularly,—the caps and bases octagonal. There is no triforium nor clerestory. The north and south aisles have in the 1, 2, 4, 5, bays,—a window of three trefoiled lights, with three trefoils in head;— I should have taken them for Middle-pointed, with inferior tracery, had I not already known the date of the church. The third bays on each side are occupied by the chapels; these date from about 1510, but have been thoroughly spoilt. The west door is curious. It contains the arms of Portugal,—the Princess Eleonora, of that kingdom, having married Frederick IV,—under this the Styrian Panther,—then the Austrian arms, with the Founder's well-known device, A. E. I. O. U. The tower is very poor and ugly; the old one was nearly pulled down in 1651,—and the present copper thing was set up in 1663.

Graz can only reckon in the fourth class of cathedrals—with Bangor and the like,—and is certainly very uninteresting. It was founded too late to influence Styrian architecture, with which indeed it has very little in common. I must not, however, forget to mention that there is an original narthex-gallery, though now much modernised.

A little to the south of the cathedral is the mausoleum of the Emperor Ferdinand. Ecclesiologically, it has nothing interesting — a classical erection : in shape, a Latin cross,—replacing an old chapel of S. Katherine's, to which Saint the present sepulchral tomb is dedicated. The chronogram which marks the date is

ferDInanDVs seCVnDVs pIe VIXIt, pIe obIIt. that is 1637.

Besides this—Catholic hero, or infernal fiend—as you read the historians and poets of the Church, or those of its Lutheran enemy, several other members of the Imperial Royal family are here interred, but none of great interest, except the late Archduke John, the benefactor of Styria, who died the year before last. His memory is in benediction in every village and mountain farm of his dear Steiermark; and never had any man a happier domestic life than he with his beloved peasant bride, the daughter of the postmaster at Aussee. She was exceedingly lovely; but, to his eternal honour be it said, the Archduke never spoke word of love to the country girl, till he offered her left-handed marriage. Not an upland farm but he had visited, not a promising lode of iron but he was called in to examine it: a firstrate marksman, an unwearied fisherman : a most scientific miner; the monument that Styria is about to raise to him will be raised by the very heart of her peasantry. His principal amusement was chamois-hunting, and as a mountaineer, even at a late period of life, he was excelled by few. I once saw him at Prague, in the year 1851; and the kind, yet acute, face, was just what I should have expected. Not a church, not a school, was built in Styria, but his purse was largely drawn on; not a farmer had vainly invoked S. Florian against fire, not a cottager had lost his cow, but the "good Archduke" was a safe resource. *Sit anima mea cum illo!*

Hence I went to the University, built 1573-1609. It is an unseemly quadrangle of brick and stone. Great as has been the kindness I have always received in foreign libraries, that which I here experienced surpassed them all. "Name your own time, Sir," said the First Librarian, "for to-morrow, and I will give you two clever undergraduates to wait on you, and to bring you what books you want." I spent nearly a day in that cinquecento room, and the heartiness with which the young men threw themselves into my pursuits, and the courtesy with which they seemed rather to be receiving than bestowing a favour, I shall never forget. The library contains 42,000 volumes (of which 3,500 are *Incunabula*) and 7,500 MSS.

Another church which I saw was the *Pfarrkirche*. This was commenced in 1466. It has chancel, nave, north aisle, [Graz, Pfarrkirche.] and double south aisle to the latter, with modern western tower façade. The apse, apparently an imitation of that of the cathedral, is trigonal: each side has a window of three trefoiled lights. The chancel, in four bays, has elaborate vaulting. The north side is—now at least—blank; its south side has three windows of three trefoiled lights. The whole choir is wretchedly modernised. The chancel arch is identical with the vaulting—no cap or base to the piers. The nave has five bays—the westernmost being occupied by the narthex gallery. The piers, octagonal, with octagonal cap and base: in England I should have put them very early in the fifteenth century; the vaulting shafts have no cap. The open seats are arabesque; as early an example of these fixtures as I have seen on the continent. The narthex gallery, now modernised, had five bays from north to south, and two from east to west. Here we again get a dodecagonal font, the sides are slightly concave; the cover arabesque. The second south arch is lower than the other; it cannot be earlier than the beginning of the sixteenth century; the vaulting is curiously elaborate.

Graz, Franciscaner Kirche. The Franciscaner Kirche (Mariä Himmel-fahrt) is said to have been finished in 1240. Chancel, nave, two aisles to the latter, modern west tower. The apse is trigonal; each side has two Middle-pointed windows of three lights, with good early tracery. The choir, of five bays, had originally in each bay a window of three trefoiled lights, with excellent tracery. The vaulting is merely cross. The chancel, higher than the nave. The nave, though the books say nothing about it, must have been rebuilt about the fifteenth century. Of four bays the piers are octagonal, with octagonal bases, but without cap. The vaulting is extremely elaborate, but much more acute than that of this date is usually. The narthex-gallery remains; but is modernised. The tower (1639-1642), the highest in the city, is said to reach an elevation of 210 feet.

Hence to the *Ursulerinen*, an erection of 1686. While waiting before the grill for the keys (the church, for it was about noon, happened to be shut), the Assistant Superior (I believe) entered into conversation with me on the never-failing subject, sisterhoods in England. *Es ist nicht zu schön, unsere Kleidung?* she asked of their own religious habit. Having always felt that the Ursuline was one of the ugliest of habits, I could only remark that the dress was of very little consequence compared with the good deeds done in the dress. "*Und das auch wahr ist,*" she said.—The church is utterly worthless. There is a very offensive wax figure of *S, Vincentia*, one of the 11,000. Graz, Ursuliner-kirche.

We then went to the Franciscan House. The buildings are worth nothing. The kindness and courtesy we experienced were really touching. There are here eight brothers and fifteen fathers. The cloisters, which, if not beautiful, are all well contrived, are hung with the beatified saints of the order; many, whose names are less known to the universal church. The library contains 14,000 volumes; but the collection of 12mo. and 18mo. breviaries of the sixteenth and seventeenth centuries I never saw equalled. Here again, the same eagerness to show me, or rather to anticipate, what I wanted. The church was built in 1600-1602. The high altar, our conductor told us, was erected on a foundation made by the ashes of 10,000 Protestant books.

Lastly,—and concluding a good day's work—to the *Barmherzige Brüder*, the Brothers of Mercy. A very interesting institution it is; but the idea occurs every where. How much better women manage these things! There are twenty-three lay brothers, and one Priest, who is the Prior. The latter took us, with the greatest kindness, over every part of the building. The dress is a plain black cassock. Their largest infirmary contains fifty beds,— it was very clean, but so very close! They can, I believe, accommodate from 120 to 150: men, of course, only. The best arranged part was the dispensary, which was crowded with poor applicants. To me it was singularly touching to see the crucifix placed in a most prominent position before the dentist's chair. We made some little offering to the House,— on which the Prior took us in to pray before the Blessed Sacrament, in a small distinct oratory. These brethren quite took my heart,—though I still think that they, in their peculiar work, fall far short of Sisters of Mercy. The institution was founded by Maximilian of Styria (of whom there is a good portrait) in 1612; there is a list of the Priors from that time: the first came from Rome. My last hour in Graz was spent in the gardens of this house, and in discussing divers ecclesiastical questions with the Prior. "We shall meet in Heaven," said he, when we parted.

And now on again by the creeping train. The express used to run from Vienna to Trieste in about sixteen hours; the time now is twenty-four! The scenery, after passing Graz, is at first pretty; it then becomes dull, as you toil across the great Leibnitzer Feld, the only large plain in Styria; but is again most striking in the cut through the Windisch Büheln hills, where our old friend the Mur, which has been our constant companion since Leoben, takes an eastward course, and leaves us to go into Hungary. We reach Marburg at half-past eight, on a glorious moonlight night, and find tolerably comfortable quarters at the *Stadt Wien*. Here, for the only time, I saw Austrian Priests playing at billiards in a coffee room. A stroll through the city showed us a tolerable Flamboyant chapel,—and the so-called Dom (not that it is really so),—a building somewhat resembling the cathedral at Graz. Here, very early next morning, we attended mass, and saw two large schools marched off in procession to some festival in one of the villages near. The dress of the women, a handkerchief worn turban-wise, is very ugly; and the strong Vendish pronunciation reminds us that we are approaching Slavonic regions. Marburg is not an interesting place,—the population about 4,500; it is the second town in Styria. We leave by railway at eight.

From Marburg to Cilly, the scenery is tremendously grand; forty miles, I should think, of unequalled railway travelling. You plunge through mountain spurs, across ravines, over torrents, all ramifying from the great Oistra-Spitze, which belongs equally to Styria, Cariuthia, and Carniola, and which presently lifts itself up to a height of 7,500 feet, on our right. The moment we enter Carniola, and slide down the desolate valley of the Sann, beauty vanishes :—the next stations are desolation themselves. At Laybach, where we dine, the scenery improves a little; for the present we pass Adelsburg without stopping,—and soon get into that horrid limestone wilderness, the Karst. All is bleakness, barrenness, utter desolation, wildness without sublimity; white circular caverns, by the rail-side, tilled as fields. Evening comes on; a north-easterly wind, and a cloudy sky, make Prestranek station gloominess itself. Our spirits go down to zero. Presently,—it was twelve minutes past seven,—by a change as from death to life, the blue Adriatic bursts on your sight, 700 feet below you,—the train running parallel to it. There, stretching away into the purple distance, is Italy,—there, across the bay, that must be Istria; the last rays of the sun fall on the white houses of Capo d'Istria. Olive-yards, cherry-yards, vineyards, orchards, maize fields, wheat, barley, terrace up the steep descent to the Adriatic; the train, down that huge incline, speeds faster and faster; every moment the Karst shelters you better and better; you forget the weariness of the long journey in the glory of your first Italian evening. The sun sets behind—where Venice must be. The Adriatic dies into purple, into blue, into grey. The shrill whistle, and the diminished distance of the sea, tell us that we are coming in; we slacken speed,—and find ourselves in the great station of Trieste.

CHAPTER III.

TRIESTE AND AQUILEIA.

EVERY one must be struck by the marvellous solidity and grandeur of the new part of Trieste. As we walked in the bright moonlight through the Piazza della Dogana, and that del Ponte Rosso, and that della Borsa, next to the palaces of the merchant princes, the huge limestone slabs with which the streets are paved, seemed most strange to an English eye. We took up our quarters in the Hotel de la Ville; an excellent hotel. It is not particularly cheap, but every luxury you can desire may be had; and the cleanliness and civility, and honest endeavours to make you comfortable, cause me to entertain the kindest remembrances of this place, where I spent six nights. It lies opposite the quay, between the Molo de Sale, and that de S. Carlo.

We reached the city on Saturday night, and were roused next morning by the clang of some near bells. On inquiry, we found them to come from the Greek church, which stands close to the hotel, on the quay, and is easily distinguishable by its green domes. It is a handsome classical building in its way; and this is its history. Up to 1752, the Greeks in Trieste had been content to worship in the Slavonic church, of which more presently. In that year, feeling their increasing importance, they hired a house, where they assembled till 1786. They then commenced the present church, dedicated to S. Nicolas, though it was not finished till 1819, from the designs of M. Pertsch. The new communion refused from the beginning to recognise the authority of the Metropolitan of Carlstadt, and is now immediately subject to the Patriarch of Constantinople. The congregation was good, and apparently, for the most part, of the upper classes. The beauty of the women was very striking. My companion had never before attended at an Eastern liturgy, and his admiration must have been very gratifying to the priests, who afterwards came to make our acquaintance.

The Slavonic church dates from 1751. It has nothing ecclesiogically remarkable.

I am not about to write a description of Trieste; and shall confine myself to its one ecclesiological curiosity, the Cathedral of S. Justus. I am bound, however, to express my warmest thanks to our excellent consul, Charles Raven, Esq., for the unwearied assistance he gave us in carrying out our plans; and more especially in forwarding our letters while we were in Dalmatia and Montenegro.

The cathedral stands on an abrupt hill above the old city. It is scarcely possible to describe its present condition, without entering first into its history.

On the temple of Capitoline Jove, it would seem that, in the fourth century (say the Tergestine antiquarians) a Basilic was erected, part of which still exists.

Of this church remain,—

The Apse;
The Baptistery;
The central part of the Nave;
And—though not so early—the mosaics.

In the sixth or seventh century, another church was built close to this, for the relics of the patron saints; this was cruciform, with central dome.

Of this church remain,—
The Apse;
Part of the Nave;
A small part of the Transept.

About 1300, these two churches were thrown into one; hence the irregular and *bizarre* appearance of the present builing. I proceed to describe it:

It has Chancel;
Nave;
Double aisles on each side;
Tower at the west end of the north aisle.

The chancel apse is circular, and much modernised; it has now a cupola. The choir has three bays. The piers are grey marble, streaked white; they are circular, have circular base on square plinth, square caps, something like our Romanesque harp caps. The easternmost arch is lower than the others.

The choir piers are distinguished from the nave piers by being raised on a soleas-step.

The mosaic represents our Lady with the DIVINE CHILD, in attitude of benediction; two angels adore.

The south aisle, that is, the second church, has an apsidal east end. In the centre is our LORD with blue mantle and cruciferous nimbus, with open book; on the right S. John, on the left, S. Servulus. The altar below appears one of great devotion. While taking some notes on a Sunday afternoon, I observed crowds of women go up to it, say a collect, kiss the figures of the saint, and retire. The apse arch is very remarkable.

Between the nave and the aisles there are eight arches, like those in the choir. Those on the south of the nave have the most decidedly Corinthian caps. The roof of the nave has the usual basilican tie. The south aisle is flat ceiled; the north aisle flat boarded. The pulpit is apparently modern, but stone; perhaps the remains of an ambon.

Over the Corinthianising caps south of the south aisle is the second cap, which we may call the Ravennat, and which I shall have occasion again to notice at Parenzo.

Outside the north wall of the nave, are four very ancient clerestory windows, with circular head, north of the north aisle.

At the east end of the south nave aisle, where the cross-arch separates it from the north chancel aisle, above that arch, on the western face, is a deeply sunk circular-headed arcade of four. The modernised chapel of S. Charles, originally named from S. Catherine of Sienna, was erected by Pius II, who had been bishop of Trieste.

At the east end of the exterior south aisle is the tomb of Don Carlos.

In the western façade is a double rose, twelve-foiled internally, twenty-four foiled externally; no doubt added when the two churches were thrown into one.

The tower has some few remains of the original heathen temple; its elevation as a campanile seems to have taken place about 1000. It had, in the middle ages, a vast wooden spire, long since destroyed by lightning. It served as a fortification, and held some small cannon as late as 1807.

The western door is made of a Roman monument cut in half.

This is as minute a description as I am able to give of a church, as difficult to describe as perhaps any I have ever seen. I now proceed with our tour.

There are few places which I have so earnestly longed to see as Aquileia; and when at length early in the month of May, we found ourselves in a capital barouche behind two excellent horses, the idea of thus visiting a church city, which seemed a mere existence of the past, had something so singular and inappropriate, as to seem an ecclesiastical joke. As at the octroi our driver gave out his destination, the whole arrangement produced the same effect in my mind as if S. Augustine had asked me to have a bottle of sodawater, or S. Jerome to procure for him a third-class ticket. But it was a lovely morning; the roads were excellent; the country glorious; and we set off in high spirits.

Our road, for some miles, ran parallel to the Vienna Railway, and gradually rose. The views, through the wood, of the Adriatic to our left, were lovely—one such glimpse I especially remember, through a plantation of almonds. Our first church was *Prosecco*—a village that gives its name to an excellent light wine. A tablet tells us that it was commenced in 1637, and consecrated *per manus Antonii Marentii, Episcopi Petenisini*, June ix, 1641.

Prosecco.

There is nothing whatever of interest. The tower is square, with double belfry windows, and octagonal stone spire.

Still keeping along the coast, in a few miles we cross the Timavus, and endeavour to get up a little classical enthusiasm. My companion is asleep: I wake him with

> Antenor potuit, mediis elapsus Achivis,
> Illyricos penetrare sinus, atque intima tutus
> Regna Liburnorum, et fontem superare Timavi:
> Unde per ora novem vasto cum murmure montis
> It mare proruptum et pelago premit arva sonanti.
> *Æn.* i. 242.

"Hoc tamen flumen obscurum hodie esse rivulum perhibent," says the Delphin commentator. By no means: it is a very respectable river; although its course from the hills, which shut out our view of the north, down to the sea, is not much more than a mile. But then, in all probability, after the manner of Carniolian rivers, Timavus has already run a considerable course on the other side of the hills, and this is only its second appearance.

But much more interesting to me is the appearance of a tolerable church close to our road; we stop, and find it to be *Duino*, otherwise *S. Giovanni* It has

Duino. chancel, nave, south tower; the whole Flamboyant. The apse is trigonal; windows of two lights trefoiled; poor tracery. Chancel, three bays: a window (apparently) originally in each, of three trefoiled lights, with clumsy tracery; only one, on south side, remains.

Sedilia, broad; circular arch cinqfoiled; good.

Vaulting of chancel curious; half classical. Execrable wall-painting; curtains with tassels.

Nave, very broad; low wooden roof, with tie beam. On north, no windows. On south, two, of three trefoiled lights. At the west end, a small rose of eight leaves.

There are only a few open seats towards the west end.

The tower is tall, thin, with two adjacent belfry windows; over this an octagonal lantern, surmounted by an octagonal spire. Over west door, 1519; which is the date of the whole church.

I copied two monuments:—

> Nobilis vir Jeorgis Reichenburg, 1530; in festo
> S. Andreæ, Ap. et Mart.

And

> Hæc requies R. D. Joh. Bapt. Marciul, parochi et Archidiaconi
> S. Joannis, 1687.

On two stones behind the altar is this inscription :—

> Ossa beatorum sunt hic inclusa piorum,
> Baptistæ Christi, simul alteriusque Johannis.
> Hic sunt conjuncti meritis et munere digni
> Stephanus et Blasius: nec non Georgius almus:
> Atque* manufortis Laurentius additur illis.
> Hos hic Germani quondam sollertia clari

---

* The poet is referring to the Sequence on S. Laurence, which begins—
> Laurenti, David magni Martyr, milesque fortis,
>   Tu imperatoris tribunal,
>   Tu manus tortorum cruentas
> Sprevisti, secutus desiderabilem, atque *manufortem.*

Manufortis is the mediæval explanation of David, as typically attributed to our Blessed LORD.

Hungaricum regem formidans valde furentem,
Jusserat abscondi magno studioque recondi.
Sic per quingentos vel forsitan amplius annos,
Non potuit sciri fuerint quâ parte locata.
Sed Udalrici Patris omnipotentis amici
Pontificis summi lenis nimiumque benigni,
Per lacrymas multas, quas Christo fudit ad aras,
Atque per immensos studuit qua pasceret urbes,
Tempore sunt ossa Sanctorius jure reperta.
Qui sanctos coluit, se sicque colendo locavit,
Quod jam cum sanctis maneat sibi vita perennis.

Monfalcone. An hour more and we enter the little town of *Monfalcone*. The church is utterly worthless. The jolly landlord of the Leone d'Oro offers himself as our companion to Aquileia, promising to be our guide to its curiosities. Our driver assents. Our new friend's very pretty wife talks a little Slavonic with me while her husband prepares himself for his expedition. We order coffee and a fowl against our return. In three or four miles we reach *Begliano*.

The church is modern. And now we come to a thick wood. The ground, however, is a complete beach of pebbles. An odd effect—the deep foliage above, the stoney waste below. Presently we see before us a milkwhite stream. It is the Isonza—here as broad as the Thames at Twickenham. A horse ferry carries us across; and now, our driver says, we are nearly in. Presently the tall tower of—yes! it is really Aquileia!—shows itself a little to our left. We get on at our best pace through Fiumicello, and at last drew up at the Leone d'Oro in Aquileia itself.

And now to the cathedral. But before we go thither, let me remind the reader of the general outline of the ecclesiastical history of Aquileia.

The Gospel is said to have been preached here by S. Mark. His disciple, S. Hermachoras, was the first bishop. In the Aquileian Missal* he is celebrated on February 12, with a proper sequence, which commences :—

> Plebs fidelis Hermachorae
> Gratuletur in honore:
> De quo Marci successore
> Gaudet Aquileïa.

Seven bishops succeeded him ; the line of archbishops commenced with S. Valerianus in A.D. 369. After the fifth Œcumenical Council, Aquileia put itself at the head of the malcontents, and its prelates, taking the title of Patriarch, commenced a schism which lasted 141 years. Paulinus, A.D. 557, was the first of these; he had ten successors. Peter I, in 698, returned to the Communion of the Church, and was allowed to retain the Patriarch title, which the schismatics had assumed.

But in the meanwhile, as a make-weight against the schismatical church, Grado had been raised, in 607, to the Patriarchate,—and sixty-nine prelates sat in that see till 1450, when it was transferred to Venice. Sixty-four catholic Patriarchs sat at Aquileia, —the last, Daniel, of Delfino, died in 1751. On this the Patriarchate was divided into the archbishoprics of Gorz, and that of Udine. Both had sundry changes.

Gorz had two archbishops; then two bishops,—the last of these took the title of Metropolitan of the

* Venetiis, ex officinâ Gregorii de Gregorius. 1519.

kingdom of Illyria, which his successor retains. Udine had five archbishops; was then reduced to a simple bishopric, but again has archiepiscopal dignity.

The present cathedral was consecrated in the year 1031, by the Patriarch Poppo, who sat from 1019—1042, and possessed great influence with the Emperor Henry II. Two inscriptions remain with respect to this consecration. I will give them here, before proceeding to describe the church.

(Modern.)

DEO DEI FILIO UNICO VIVO ET VERO JESU CHRISTO ET SUÆ BEATISSIMÆ GENITRICI SEMPER VIRGINI ALMÆ MARIÆ SUIS QUE SANCTIS MARTYRIBUS HERMACHORÆ PONT. ET FORTUNATO HUJUS SANCTI TEMPLI SACERDOTI.

(Ancient.)

✢ ANNO DOMCÆ ICARNATIOIS MXXXI INDICTIONE X III ID. JVL. PRÆSIDE DOMIO JOHAN. XVIII PAPA VRBIS ROMÆ IMPANTE CHONRADO IMPATORE AVGVSTO IMPII SVI ANNO V CONSTRVCTV CONSECRATV E HOC TEMPLVM IN HONORE SCÆ DEI GENETRICIS ET PPETVÆ VIRGINIS MARIÆ SCORQ MARTYR. HERMACHORÆ ET FORTVNATI A DNO POPONE VENERABILI PATRIARCHA AQVILEIENS . PARITERQVE DVOB ROMANI PONTIFICATVS . VIDELICET JOANE STÆ ROMANE ECCLIE EPISCOPO CARDINALI . ET DODONE . S.TE ROMANE . ECCLI⁻E . EPISCOPO . CARDINALI . ALISQ COEPISCOPIS . SCILICET . ADALGERIO . TERGESTINO . IOHANNE . POLENSI . WOLDALRICO . PETENENT; AZONE . CIVITATIS . NOVE . PVODEBERTO . CONCORDIEN ; ROTHARIO . TARVISIANO . AYSTVLFO . PATAVINO . WODALRICO . BRIXIANO . IIERMA .... BELLVENEN; REGISONE . FELTREN . WODALRICO . TRIDENTINO . ET . HELMEGERO . CENENTEN ; IN . DNO . FELICITER.

EGO POPO IIVIUS AQVILEIENSIS ECCLESIÆ PATRIARCHA, VNA CVM DVOB. ROM. EPISCOPIS CARDINALIBVS, ET XII COEPISCOPIS PRÆSIDENTE DOMINO IOANNE PAPA XIX ET IMPERATORE CONRADO AVGVSTO, CONSECRAVI HOC TEMPLVM IN HONOREM S. MARIÆ GENITRICIS DEI ET SANCTORVM MARTYRVM HERMACORÆ ET FORTVNATI . OB CVIVS SOLEMNITATEM IDEM ROM. SVM .

PONTIFEX DE GRATIA APOSTOLICA CONCESSIT INDVLGENTIAM C. ANNORVM, ET C. DIERVM SINGVLIS ANNIS OMNIBVS VERE POENITENTIBVS, ET CONFESSIS DICTAM ECCLESIAM VISITANTIBVS CAVSA DEVOTIONIS, ET IN FESTO DICTORVM MARTYRVM HERMACORÆ ET FORTVNATI, ET PER OCTAVAS EORVM SINGVLIS DIEBVS XVIII ANNORVM, ET TOTIDEM QVADRANTENARVM . ITEM DICTI CARDINALES AVCTORITATE APOSTOLICA, OB REVERENTIAM S . QVIRINI MARTYRIS, QVI EIVS CORPVS PORTAVERVNT DE VRBE, ET CONDIDERVNT A PARTE DEXTERA IN ALTARI PARVO IVXTA ALTARE MAIVS, ET OB REVERENTIAM B . M . PAPÆ, ET CONFESSORIS, CVIVS ETIAM CORPVS DE VRBE PORTAVERVNT, ET COLLOCAVERVNT A SINISTRA IN ALTARI PARVO IVXTA MAIVS ALTARE CONCESSERVNT INDVLGENTIAM X ANNORVM ET X QVADRAGENARVM TVM IN SVPRADICTIS SOLEMNITATIBVS, QVAM ETIAM IN FESTIVITATIBVS . . . . . .

The names of the sees, mentioned in the second inscription, will be found explained in the next chapter but one.

The minute description of the cathedral I leave for an appendix, by which time I hope to be able to present the reader with a ground plan of it, which has not yet reached me.

Chapter IV.

THE GLAGOLITA RITE.

I have said that one cause of my tour was an earnest desire of examining for myself the Glagolita rite. It will be well that I should dwell on its nature and history in the first place,—the rather that I cannot entirely agree, either on the one hand with its Latin supporters, as Ginzel and Berčič,* nor on the other with its Greek opponents, as Dr. Pavsky.

Every one knows that the gospel was first preached about the year 863, by S.S. Cyril and Methodius, in Moravia, under the auspices of the Emperor Michael III, and at the instance of the Princes Rostiloff and Sviatopolk. They, but chiefly S. Cyril, found the Slavonic a formed language, but invented an alphabet for it.—hence called the Cyrillic,—the same with that which we call Slavonic, and the parent of the modern Russ character.

Into this language, and this character, they translated the office books of the *Eastern* Church. It is

---

* It will be well to inform the reader that, in Illyrian,—
s is sounded as English *s*.
c ,, ,, ,, *ts*.
š ,, ,, ,, *sh*.
č ,, ,, ,, *tch*.
z ,, ,, ,, *z*.
ž ,, ,, ,, *zh* (French *j*.)

in vain that Ginzel,* to whose pages I must refer the reader, endeavours to show that the liturgy translated by these Apostles of the Slavonic tongue was the Latin; the arguments of Dobroffsky and others must convince every unprejudiced person, what, indeed, common sense would seem to teach, that Oriental Missionaries introduced the Oriental rite.

The rite then was Greek; the language, Slavonic; the character, Cyrillic.† But Cyril was soon taken from the scene of his labours. Called to Rome for certain explanations regarding his diocese, he there slept in the LORD, February 14, 868. His friend and companion, Methodius, was then, by the Pope, raised to the dignity of Archbishop of the Moravians,—and returning to his own province, he continued the good work with zeal. However, he had enemies, and their complaints ere long reached Rome. A brief, addressed by Pope John VIII to "Methodius, the most reverend Archbishop of the Pomeranian Church," and dated June 14, 879, accuses him, in the first place, of preaching doctrines not in accordance with those of the Roman Church; and continues thus:—

"We have heard, too, that you sing masses in a barbarous language, namely the Slavonian. Whence we have already, in our letters directed to you by Paul, Bishop of Ancona, prohibited you from solemnizing the rites of mass in that tongue; but either in the Latin or the Greek, as the Church of GOD, dispersed through the whole world, and spread abroad

---

* Geschichte der Slawen Apostel Cyril u. Method. Leitmeritz, 1857, pp. 107—112.

† Ginzel denies this: but see after.

among all nations, is wont to do. You may, however, employ that language in preaching or speaking to the people, since the Psalmist exhorts all nations to praise GOD, and the Apostle would have every tongue confess that JESUS is LORD, to the glory of GOD the FATHER." The archbishop is, therefore, commanded to come to Rome,—and a Papal letter of the same date, to Sviatopluk, Duke of Moravia, gives a similar requisition. Accordingly, Methodius went to Rome.

In the following June (880), the Pope had changed his opinion. We have a letter of that date, addressed to Sviatopluk, containing the highest praises of Methodius. The Pontiff informs that Prince, that he had, as requested, consecrated one Victrin to be Bishop of Nitria in Moravia, and was ready to consecrate a third when asked, so that the canonical number required for keeping up the apostolic succession might be furnished by Moravia itself. And then he continues,—and this is the part with which we are more especially concerned:—

"As to the Slavonic letters invented by Constantine the Philosopher, in which the praises of GOD rightly resound, we highly commend them; and we exhort that, in the same language, the doctrine and works of CHRIST our LORD shall still be set forth. For Holy Scripture commands us to glorify GOD, not in three tongues only, but in all languages; as it is written "O praise the LORD, all ye heathen: laud Him, all ye people." * * * * * Nor does it in any way affect the sacred doctrine, and the true faith, to sing masses in the same Slavonic tongue, or to read the

Sacred Gospel and the Divine lection of the Old and New Testament, or to render the other offices in that tongue, so they be well translated and interpreted; seeing that He Who created the three principal languages, that is to say, Hebrew, Greek, and Latin, created also all others to His honour and glory. Nevertheless, we direct, that, in all the churches of your realm, for the greater decency, the Gospel be first read in Latin, and then translated in Slavonic in the ears of the people, who understand not the Latin tongue; as we hear is already done in some places. And should it be more agreeable to you and to your judges, you are at liberty to hear mass in the Latin tongue alone.

Methodius died the death of the righteous in 885, —and I am not now concerned to pursue further the history of the Moravian Church. We turn to our more immediate subject.

The South-Western Slavs were the first of that family to receive the Gospel. In the seventh century, the Servs, Croatians, Dalmatians, and Istrians, had in large numbers, under their Prince Paga,* given their names to Christ. The destruction of Salona by heathen Slavs, in A.D. 639, rendered Pope John IV, (639—641), himself a native of Salona, all the more eager for the evangelization of his native land; and when that good Pontiff was taken from the world, his successor continued anxious for the success of the holy scheme. Martin I (649—653), raised the new city Spalato, rising as it were from the ruins of

* Asseman. Kalendar, ii, 294.

Salona, to an archiepiscopate. Henceforward the Latin rite took firm hold of Dalmatia.

But when Basil (867—896), in the time when Cyril and Methodius had commenced their holy warfare, had ascended, himself a Slav, the Byzantine Throne, he naturally wished that the Oriental rite should prevail in Dalmatia, and hence arose a vigorous contest between the east and west; and the Oriental rite, in the Slavonic letters of Cyril, was in many places adopted.

In A.D. 925*—that is, only forty years after the final approbation bestowed by John VIII on the use of the Slavonic as an ecclesiastical language, and his commendation of Methodius, we find the following brief from John X to John of Salona and his suffragans. After dwelling on the *Tu es Petrus*, he continues:—

"But GOD forbid that they who worship CHRIST should forsake the doctrine of the Gospel, the volumes of the Canons, and the Apostolic precepts, and should fly to the teaching of Methodius, whose name we have never seen in any copy of the sacred authors. * * * * So that, according to the custom of the Roman church, no one, in the Slavonian territory, should perform the sacrifice of the mass in any other language but the Latin; and because the Slavs are the most special sons of the Roman Church, they ought to remain in the doctrine of their mother." He then gives commission for the uprooting the "evil plant" to John of Spalato, John of Ancona, and Leo of

---

* Farlati, Illyr. Sacr. iii. 93.

Præneste. At the same time he wrote to Tamislaff, King of the Croats, and to his Zupans, to assist the ecclesiastics with the civil arm.

No doubt it was the introduction of the Oriental rite, in Cyrillic characters and Slavonic language, which rendered the Pope so inveterate against the use of that character and these letters in the Roman rite. Besides, it involved a translation of Missal and Breviary; no easy task in the most learned of ages, an enormous labour then. The National Council of Spalato* (A.D. 925), by its tenth Canon (which, however, has come down to us in a corrupted state), absolutely forbade the use of Slavonic in future, except in case of extreme necessity, and then only by priests already ordained. The canon gave rise to deep discontent, and sent many and many a Dalmatian to find a vernacular within the Eastern church; and not a few, it is to be feared, to the loathsome heresy of the Paterenes, then abounding in Bosnia.

For 140 years, nevertheless, partly connived at, partly secreting itself, the rite struggled on. About 1064 the Cardinal Archbishop Maynard held another Provincial Council at Spalato, in which those who should employ it were to be delivered over to an anathema. The poor Slav priests made an earnest but ineffectual appeal to Alexander II. He told them, what the council had said before, that Methodius was a heretic, and added, that he was an Arian; affirmed that the Cyrillic letters were Arian letters; that he could not have Arian letters in his church;

* Farlati, Illyr. Sacr. iii, 97.

and that they must observe what his venerable brother Maynard had enjoined, or it would be the worse for them. This depends on the testimony of Thomas, who was then Archdeacon of Spalato, and who seems to have had a fellow feeling with the appellants. He tells us of the great grief caused by the Pope's decision.

But, in 1248 another attempt was made. Innocent IV was entreated to allow the performance of the Roman offices in the Slavonic language, but not in the Cyrillic character. No; "in a certain character invented by S. Jerome" (who, the reader will remember, was a Dalmatian) and known as the Glagolita, from the Slavonic *Glagol'*, "a word." Before saying anything of this character, I will give the two Slavonic alphabets, Glagolita and Cyrillic.

Now, there are three opinions with regard to the Glagolita:

1. That it is the primitive Slavonic character, and therefore far older than the Cyrillic. This is the general western view.

2. That, by a pious fraud, some clever priest, wishing to obtain the Pope's sanction to the Slavonic Liturgy, invented this character, to render the employment of the vernacular possible, without the adjunct of the hated Cyrillic. This was Dobroffsky's theory, and is followed by most Easterns.

3. That it was invented by Cyril for his Latin, as the other for his Greek, converts. This seems Ginzel's view, and it has, I believe, few followers. The first is decidedly my own opinion, and I proceed to give my reasons.

Glagolitic value	Glagolitsa-Slavonic	Power	Cyrillo-Slavonic	Cyrillic value
1	Ⰰ	a	А	1
2	Ⰱ	b	Б	
3	Ⰲ	v	В	2
4	Ⰳ	g	Г	3
5	Ⰴ	d	Д	4
6	Ⰵ	e	Є	5
7	Ⰶ	French j	Ж	
8	Ⰷ	z	Ѕ	6
9	Ⰸ	zh	З	7
10	Ⰹ	e	И	8
20	Ⰺ	i	І / (Й)	10
30	Ⰻ	i		
40	Ⰼ	English j		
40	Ⰽ	k	К	20
50	Ⰾ	l	Л	30
60	Ⰿ	m	М	40
70	Ⱀ	n	Н	50
80	Ⱁ	o	О	70
90	Ⱂ	p	П	80
100	Ⱃ	r	Р	100
200	Ⱄ	s	С	200
300	Ⱅ	t	Т	300
400	Ⱆ	u	ОУ	
500	Ⱇ	f	Ф	500

Glagolitic value	Glagolitsa-Slavonic	Power	Cyrillo-Slavonic	Cyrillic value
600	Ⱈ	guttural ch	Х	600
700	Ⱉ	long o	Ѡ	800
800	Ⱋ	sht	Щ	
900	Ⱌ	ts	Ц	900
1000	Ⱍ	tsh	Ч	
	Ⱎ	sh	Ш	
	Ⱏ	mute o *	Ъ	
	Ⱔ	yi *	ЪН / Ы	
	Ⱐ	mute e *	Ь	
	Ⱑ Ⱘ	ya *	Ѣ (Ꙗ) / (Ѣ)	
	Ⱓ	yu *	Ю	
			Ѩ	
			Ѥ	
			Ѧ	
			Ѫ	90
			Ѩ	
			Ѭ	
		x	Ѯ	60
		ps	Ѱ	700
		th	Ѳ	9
		y	Ѵ	400

* These, and the ensuing Cyrillic letters, have sounds that cannot be expressed in any character.

I. The extraordinary clumsiness of the Glagolita—for in the modern Alphabet, as I have given it, that clumsiness has been very much lessened,—would have made it an Herculean task to write out a Missal or Breviary in it. Why did not the missionaries, who must have had a certain amount of talent, frame, supposing it framed by them, an easy running character, instead of one so painfully laborious?

II. If we examine the two alphabets together, we shall see that some letters are the same. Which are they?

Look at the theory of Cyril. He first took the Greek alphabet, and used it up. He then had, somehow or other, to procure a set of signs for sounds not Greek, principally *sh*, *tsh*, *zh*, and *dj*, and for the soft beautiful mutes *yer*, *yier*, and *yere*. Now these are the very characters in which his alphabet coincides with the Glagolita. If Cyril's were the later of the two, how very natural that he should avail himself of already existing Slavonic letters for expressing Slavonic sounds! But if the Glagolita were the later, why should its author invent for himself those characters which were common to the Greek and the Cyrillic, but copy all those which were peculiar to the Cyrillic as distinguished from the Greek? Is not this the very opposite of what he would have done? He might, to save trouble, have taken the Greek, or at least the Latin characters, so far as they served his turn: but the special Cyrillic letters are those which he would specially have avoided.

I observe also, that there is a striking resemblance between some of the Sanscrit and some of the Glagolita types; a thing which could not, in that age, have arisen from a Dalmatian Priest possessing any acquaintance with Sanscrit, and which can surely never be attributed to chance.

As to Ginzel's hypothesis, it is only founded on one argument, that the characters condemned by Alexander II, are called Cyrillic. But he takes them to have been Glagolita. Deny, as we unhesitatingly do, this belief,—and he has no other reason to allege. And even were this opinion correct, how easily might those who thought Methodius an Arian heretic, have also, with as little truth, thought him to be the author of the Glagolita! Dr. Ginzel adds, that the form of the Glagolita is easier to a hand accustomed to write Latin than is Cyrillic; if he had copied even only as much as I have done of the two, he would, and that speedily, retract his opinion.

Innocent IV was applied to by the Bishop of Zengh, where, I suppose, the feeling was strongest, for permission to celebrate in the vernacular tongue. His brief is not only extremely sensible, but expressed with great neatness. "Nos igitur attendentes, ut sermo rei, et non res sermoni subjecta, licentiam tibi in illis duntaxat partibus, ubi de consuetudine observantur præmissa, dummodo ex ipsius varietate literæ sententia non lædatur, auctoritate præsentium confirmamus." It is dated at Lyons, March 19, 1248.

This brief gave, of course, a great impulse to the transcription of Glagolita service books; and nothing is more certain, than that this character and the Cyrillic were frequently used together. Such a MS. is the *Codex*, published by Kopitar, known as the Texte du Sacre, because formerly employed in the consecration of the Kings of France at Rheims. Of this, the first thirty-two pages are Cyrillic; the last sixty-six, Glagolita. The former portion is said to have been written by S. Procopius; the latter is dated 1395.

Early Glagolita MSS. are of the extremest rarity. A fragment of the 9th or 10th century exists in the Capitular Library at Prague; it is a translation of some of the Greek offices for Good Friday. This yields another argument against the Roman invention of the character. It is in a good bold hand; but the letters are more rounded than they are at present cast. The *Codex Clozianus*, the most celebrated of all, on which Kopitar published a work at Vienna in 1836, and which is now at Trent, contained all (but now a part only) of the Bible, and some sermons of S. Chrysostom. The character is small and round; very difficult to read. The very learned Miklošić considers this the oldest of all. There is another (eleventh century) of the gospels, which was once at Athos, and is now at Kazan; and a similar one of the same date in the monastery, called Zograph, in Macedonia. A Praxapostolus of the twelfth, in the church of *S. Clement* of Okhrida. All these are of the Greek rite,—and of the rounded shape. I think it might be gathered that the round character belongs to the Oriental, the square to the Western MSS. At Birbino, in Isola Lunga (of which more presently) Berčić discovered a very curious fragment of a Breviary (twelfth century), and another at Tkon, in the island Pasman. A fine Breviary was written at Zengh, in 1359, and is now in the possession of

Prince Lobkovitch, at Prague. A Missal of 1368 is at Vienna. A Pasmanian Breviary, very curious, which belongs to Canon George Batchinstok, parish priest of Pasman, is of the fourteenth century. Father Berčič, who explored all the islands for Glagolita fragments, and incorporated his researches in the Chrestomathia linguæ Veteroslovenicæ, to which I am very much indebted, possesses more than sixty different fragments anterior to the fifteenth century.

I now come to the printed editions.

The *Editio Princeps* of the Glagolita Missal is that which appeared in Venice, A.D. 1483, but where it was printed is unknown. It is a very good square character. This is one of the rarest of books; I only *know* of one copy, at Vienna; but, I believe, there are one or two others. The *Editio Princeps* of the Cyrillic Liturgy did not appear till 1519; also at Vienna.

The *second* edition of the Glagolita Missal,—Zengh, 1507. This has a small round type. A ritual was printed at the same place and time.

The *third*, Venice, 1528. Fr. Paul de Modrussa, a Franciscan, was editor.

The *fourth*, at Fiume, 1531. Simeon Kozhitchitch, Bishop of Modrussa, a native of Zara, supplied the funds.

The *fifth*, (an abbreviated edition, and prefixed to the Breviary), Venice, 1562. The editor was Nicolas Brozhitch, parish priest of Castelmuschio, in Veglia: (in Illyrian it is Omishel) and the Latinised form, Castromusculum.

For seventy years there was no further edition of the Missal. Whether the Pontiffs, in that interval, were really opposed to the licence, or whether the state of Europe entirely turned their thoughts from the poor Slavs, I know not; but the want of books became excessive. Ferdinand II received a strong remonstrance from the Priests of the Illyrian Rite, that their flocks would not attend the Latin mass, and were in the habit of going to the Eastern churches, where they heard their own Slavonic. At length, Urban VIII resolved to remedy the evil, and the *sixth* edition of the Glagolita Missal appeared at Rome, under the care of Raphael Levákovitch, of Veglia,—a man altogether unqualified for the task. However, Urban VIII, by an apostolic letter of November 29, 1630, approved the edition, and enjoined its use to the exclusion of all former Missals.

The *seventh* edition appeared at Rome in 1708; the editor was John Pastrici, priest of Spalato. But he unfortunately, was not much better qualified for his work than Levákovitch had been. He says himself, in writing to the Dalmatian Bishops, on this subject—" When I was a boy of seven, I left my country for Venice, and after that fixed myself at Rome. With the characters named from S. Jerome I had been well acquainted from my infancy; but from thence till my fifty second year, I had had time enough almost to forget them. Whence I had to brush up my own learning, and thought it better to keep close to the old books."

In 1741, another edition was called for. Rome was certainly unfortunate. The Archbishop of Zara, the illustrious Vincent Zmaievitch, recommended Matthew Karaman, a priest of his own diocese, as the fittest person for the work, and it was entrusted to him. But unhappily, he had resided for several years at S. Petersburg, and had there become acquainted with modern Russ, which he took to be the old church Slavonic, and had imbibed the idea, that the nearer he could bring the Illyrian dialect to the latter, the purer he would make it. Hence he produced a work, which was not only offensive to the Dalmatians, as obnoxious to the charge of being Russian; but has had a materially bad influence on the language. To give an example that every one can understand. The old Slavonic preposition for *in* is *v*'. In Russ this is now changed to *vo*, in Illyrian to *va*. Levakovitch had given the formula of the sign of the Cross correctly enough; *va ime' Otza*, &c. Karaman caused great offence by printing *vo imja' Otza*. However, his work was approved by four Russian church ecclesiastics (the very persons who ought not to have been consulted), and finally was authorized by Benedict XIV, August 15, 1754. In this the Pope expressly forbade the practice, then beginning to prevail of printing the every day portions of the mass in Roman letters. Karaman, as the reward of his labours, succeeded Zmaievitch at Zara.

I now come to the Breviary.

The *Editio Princeps* is that of Venice, 1562; edited by the same Nicolas Brozhitch of Castelmuschio of whom we have spoken before. The alterations made by Pius V, and Clement VIII, and Urban VIII, in compliance with the Canon of the Council of Trent, made another Illyrian edition necessary. This was first put into the hands of Levakovitch of whom I have spoken before; and he was associated with Cyril Terletzky,

—the notorious deviser of the Slavonic *Unia*—Russian Bishop of Chelm. The result was, that the Breviary was full of Russisms, and not only so, but in some words showed a deficiency of Slavonic learning altogether. Take one example:—the proper word for temptation is *napast;* but a modern Russism made it *iskušenye,* which to Dalmatian ears meant *attempt.* However, Terletzky thought that being the Russ, it was also the old Slavonic expression; and the 6th petition of the Lord's Prayer, which up to this time had stood

I ne uwedi nas wnapast,

he gave

I ne w-wedi nas w-iskušenije.

which, in Dalmatian meant,—"and lead us not into an attempt." But had Terletzky only taken the trouble to look at the great Ostrog Bible of 1581, the standard of printed old Slavonic, he would have found the word *napast,* which he rejected as Dalmatian, standing in the Lord's Prayer. However, this translation was authorized by Innocent X; it appeared in 1648, and Levakovitch, as his recompense, was made Bishop of Okhrida (Prima Justiniana) in Bulgaria.

The *second* edition then is this, Rome, 1648.

The *third,* Rome, 1688, under the editorship of Pastrici, who acquitted himself no better here than in the Missal.

The *fourth* and last, Rome, 1791. This is edited by John Peter Gocinić, Bishop of Arbe, with the help of Karaman; and it is that which is usually found in the Glagolitic churches. It is a rather handsome octavo, large and long in proportion to its size, and forms two volumes.

There have also been editions of the Ritual, but in the Roman character. In 1640, a handsomely printed book in small quarto, was edited by Bartholomew Cassius; dedicated to Pope Urban VIII, and approved by him. Here Roman characters are alone employed, and there is not even an attempt at expressing the peculiar Slavonic letters further than by the ç for *tch*. It is a handsomely printed book, the rubrics in red; the music very boldly and clearly printed on red lines. But barbarous as Slavonic must always look when expressed in Latin characters, it is more barbarous than ever here from the peculiar method of spelling employed. Benedict XIV by his brief of August 15, 1754, forbade in future the employment of any character except Glagolita for ecclesiastical Slavonic. But this brief was a dead letter from the beginning; no Glagolita ritual ever appeared, and Cassian's translation, therefore, continued to be used till 1791, when an improved edition, but still in Latin character, was put forth by authority.

Within the last few years, indeed, a further step has been taken in the same direction. The Epistles and Gospels, the proper Prefaces, the office for Holy Week, &c., and the Sequences, were printed in 1857, in the Latin character, and received the imprimatur of the Bishop of Spalato. From this book I have more than once seen the Gospel read during mass. A remarkable peculiarity in it is this—that, whereas, as every one knows, there is no sequence in the Roman

Missal for Christmas Day, an original Illyrian one is here given, and is, as I am told, a great favourite with the people. I inquired in the Bishop's court at Selenico, how this publication could be reconciled with the Apostolic letter of Benedict XIV. To which the answer was: that, had Benedict XIV been as well acquainted with the wants of Dalmatia as its present prelates, he would have been the first to sanction such a publication; a remark, which I doubt not, is true enough.

Besides the writers I have already mentioned, the only others in Glagolita are two or three editions of spelling books—Azbukvidars as they are called.

It now only remains to compare the extent to which the Glagolita office was employed when first permitted, with its use at the present day.

In the chapter on Ecclesiastical Dalmatia, the reader will be told that that province now forms one archbishopric, namely, Zara; with six suffragans. But in the time of Innocent IV, when the ecclesiastical employment of Slavonic was first allowed, it contained four archbishoprics; namely, Zara, Spalato, Ragusa, Antivari, and twenty-seven bishoprics. In all of these, it would seem to have been, if not universal, at all events very general; while in the other four bishoprics of Istria, namely, Trieste, Capo d'Istria, Citta Nova, and Parenzo, it was also common. So it was in Bosnia, Servia, and Bulgaria. In the diocese of Zara, and in those of Arbe, Ossero, and Veglia, every single church was Glagolitic, except the cathedrals. In Spalato, out of thirty-six parishes, only eight were Latin. As late as 1733, nineteen churches in the diocese of Parenzo employed the Slavonic rite. Zengh was the only cathedral of which I can find it absolutely stated that its services were vernacular.

Far different is the state of things at the present day. In the first place, the negligence which, from 1531 to 1631, left the Illyrian priests without an edition of their missal, drove many worshippers to embrace the Latin rite; many to the Greek Church; and some, I was assured on the spot, though it seems hard to believe, to the remnant of the Patarenes, who even then clung, as their last refuge, to the wild mountains of Bosnia. Afterwards, when Levakovitch brought out his edition, its corruptions rendered it very unpopular. People did not like to be told to pray —as I have said was the case—" Lead us not into an *attempt*." And so, day by day, and partly also no doubt from the greater facilities of intercourse with foreign nations, the Latin rite usurped on the Glagolita, till the latter was reduced to its present dimensions.

	Parishes.	Souls.	Convents.	Priests in Convents.
Diocese of Veglia.				
Veglia Island	13	14,283	3	9
Cherso Island	—	—	1	1
Diocese of Zara.				
Deanery of Zara	7	8,075	1	2
,, Nona	4	1,793		
,, Rasanze	1	329		
,, Novograd	4	967		
,, Albaemaris	1	180		
,, Selbe	14	6,330		
,, S. Euphemia	9	4,536		
	40	22,210		

Diocese of Spalato.	Parishes.	Souls.	Convents.	Priests in Convents.
Deanery of Spalato	10	9,963		
„ Trau	1	320		
„ Segni	19	11,597		
„ Makarska	3	3,077		
„ Neretva	6	3,687		
„ Imotschi	8	5,572		
„ Almissa	15	6,296		
	62	40,512		
Diocese of Sebenico.	3	2,077		
TOTAL :—Veglia	13	14,283		
Zara	40	22,210		
Spalato	62	40,512		
Sebenico	3	2,077		
	118	79,082		

So it will be observed, that the vernacular use has utterly died even at Istria, where, 150 years ago, it was the language of the ecclesiastical majority.

It may be interesting, as an example of the fluctuation of the translation, and its orthography, to compare a hymn from the Ritual of 1640, with the epistles and gospels of 1858.

> Gloria, laus et honor tibi sit, Rex Christe, Redemptor!
> Cui puerile decus prompsit Hosanna pium.
> Israel es tu Rex, Davidis et inclyta Proles,
> Nomine qui Domini, Rex benedicte, venis.

(1640.)

Slavvà, hyàla, i cast tebbi buddi Kràgliu Isùkarste od kupittegliu,
Kòmu ditinska dijka pievva Hosanna millo.

Izraelski tij kragl, Davidov plèmenit plood:
Koyi ù imme Gospòdinovo Kragl blagossovglieni prihòdisc.

(1858.)

Slavati, fàla, çast Karste Spasiteglju;
Kòm ùst ditinski slàst pivà: Hoxana xelju.
Israela Kràglsi, kavi çastnà Davida:
U ime priscaosi Gospodgnè sudà.

Chapter V.

ISTRIA.

We started from Trieste for a tour through Istria. As there is a post road as far as Parenzo, and a road which is perfectly carriageable from thence to Pola, we engaged a carriage with two horses in Trieste, and a servant who was recommended to us as being able to speak the various Illyrian dialects of Slavonic, as well as Italian, German, French, and English. And Giuseppe Dundich, for that was his name, proved himself a most trustworthy courier both in our Istrian, and afterwards in our Dalmatian tour. He had spent some years in the service of the English ambassadors in Persia; and was well acquainted with India and China, though long settled at Trieste, of which he is a native.

The way lies through the eastern quarter of Trieste and passes the three cemeteries, Greek, Latin, and Protestant; they occupy a lovely situation on the slope of a hill, which forms the northern horn of a little bay, blue with all the blueness of the Adriatic. The road skirts the sea-coast for some miles; then cuts across a well-cultivated headland, and the beautiful gulf of Capo d'Istria opens out at once. A quaint, crowded, mediæval town, Capo d'Istria occupies a little promontory; narrow streets, alleys that, from one end to the other form only a flight of steps, an ill-paved fishing-quay—these take up the greater part of the city; but the cathedral stands in an open *place* with a few trees planted about it, and the episcopal gardens skirting it to the north. It is entirely modern; only in the west end some fragments of Roman inscriptions have been built up. The tower, tall, thin, and ending in a prolonged pyramid, is merely a poor copy of that adjoining S. Mark's at Venice, as are all those which I shall briefly hereafter describe as Venetian towers. The altar stands between chancel and nave; the choir is square-ended, and the stalls occupy its three sides; the bishop's throne being placed in the centre of the east end. This I take to be a radically vicious construction for a square east-end. The Synthronus, which it is intended to represent, absolutely requires an apsidal termination: then the bishop's throne obtains dignity from its very position; here it is only one stall out of a row. Nevertheless, this is a favourite Istrian and Dalmatian arrangement, more particularly in monastic churches. How early such an idea may be, I cannot say; I have seen no example previous to 1510 or 1520.

After attending vespers in the Cathedral, we next visited the Capuchin Monastery; it seems very poor, and only contains five or six brethren. They showed us, however, with the greatest courtesy, their library, the poor remains left in the devastation made by the Duke of Dalmatia, in the French invasion of 1814. But in this and many other instances, I have regretted that no ecclesiastical commission had been issued for the examination of these monastic libraries. The printed books are sometimes curious enough; and there is generally a sufficient store of *Incunabula*. But there is also, generally speaking, a MS. history, either of the monastery itself, or of the diocese, or the province; or some kindred work. Probably the greater part of such histories would be utterly unworthy of publication; but from the short glances that I was able to give to a few such, I saw that there was considerable likelihood of some curious facts, in hands that knew how to use them, being brought to light. There is, for example, in this Capuchin house at Capo d'Istria, a MS. *Historia Ecclesiæ Gradensis;* it seems to be continued for about a hundred years. I there read an account of a visit paid by Savanarola to Gortz, and of a sermon preached by him at the Great Church: a sermon which the writer seems to have heard for himself; one of those fiery discourses which raised so strong a feeling against the fearful corruption of the times, and at last brought the preacher to the stake. The whole passage would be well worth printing; and no doubt it is but one among several such.

Hence to the Observantine Convent, somewhat larger than the Capuchin. From this we continued our route along the coast: the landscape becoming flat and ugly, and our immediate view presenting nothing but a series of salt-pans; and the low white houses, and general barrenness, and desolation which accompany them. A very long, but gradual rise, brought us, about dusk, above the Promontory of Pirano. The little town lay crowded together far below us; the descent to it is so steep that we had to walk down. I thought that I had never seen anything more picturesque than the quay, and lake-like bay; and beyond the eastern hills, Montemaggiore, for example, and Monte Gasino. The clouds were piled thick and black together; and an occasional vivid flash of lightning threw tower, and street, and mast into sharp relief. But in the interval, Venus and Saturn, though close together, had each its own lovely path of light on the water, unbroken, yes, and even untrembling.—I cannot say much for our inn; but it did; and in the morning we began our explorations. In the first place to the *Cathedral*, still so called, though so no longer. It presents the ground-plan of a basilic, but is now entirely modern, with the exception of a few classical fragments built in at the west end; and the apses remain, though much modernised, towards the east. The choir is, as at Capo d'Istria, behind the high altar, and invisible from the greater part of the nave. The present structure was dedicated on S. Mark's Day, 1638; but a very curious inscription remains to tell that the original church was dedicated on S. Mark's Eve, 1344. The seven altars, it says, were consecrated by these bishops (but as more than seven prelates are mentioned, we are left in some difficulty how to explain the assertion.)

Pirano Cathedral of S. Mark. Justinopolensis (*i.e.* Capo d'Istria), Enonensis (*i.e.* Cittanova, united in 1434 to Parenzo), Parentinus, Polensis, Petenesinus (*i.e.* Pisino or Mitterburg, in the centre of Istria), Capiolanensis, Evelinensis (Buje), Domatensis, Soaralensis. These last sees I cannot explain. The cantons of Pirano, Capo d'Istria, Castelnuovo,

Buje, and Montona, now belong to the see of Capo d'Istria, which is united with Trieste; the Bishop resides half the year in each of his cathedral cities. The tower of Pirano is of Venetian idea; tall, thin, pyramidal headed, and capped with an angel,—it is visible far out at sea,—indeed, the building stands nobly, buttressed up on the very edge of a steep cliff, from which the only descent to the shore is by a precipitous staircase. To the east of the cathedral is the modern octagonal church of *S. John Baptist*, once the Baptistery; the sides retain a good deal of classical sculpture; there is a square draw-well in the middle. *S. Pietro* is a small modern church. The Franciscan Convent, of the seventeenth century, has a tolerable cloister; it contains, at present, seven priests, and three laymen. I noticed, in going over the house, that "an ancient and fish-like smell" pervaded every part of it. This was at last explained by our being introduced into the museum of Father Antonio, who, it seems, has the reputation of being one of the first German ichthyologists of his day; and who has fishermen, in different parts of Istria, in his pay. He endeavoured to interest a very unintelligent auditor in his treasures. The library is but poor; the same apology was made here as always, for its being in such wretched order. The spoliation by the French is irreparable; but surely their disorder need not have continued to this time. The Conventual Church, with a flat painted ceiling, seems to have been a favourite place of burial.

<small>S. Pietro.</small>

<small>Franciscan Church.</small>

The floor is covered with inscriptions such as this :—

Defrani soboles, mundana pericula tranans,
  Securum hic portum, quo requiescat, habet.
           1729.

S. Stephen and the *Madonna delle Salute*, a worthless modern building. And so we bade adieu to Pirano, and continued our route southward. It lay along the flat coast, salt-pans everywhere: here and there a little white chapel for the salt-workers. A clean, healthy trade; but the barrenness of the land in which it is carried on is unpleasing. The country shortly after improves; and is truly what the French call *riant*. Vineyards and oliveyards, hill and dale, the green ilex and the lime, the vine shoots trailed along the hedges, after the manner which the Portuguese call *enforcados* or *de enforcado*, amidst dog-roses and hawthorn; every copse sending up its morning hymn of praise from countless nightingales; every fleecy *lamb-cloud*, as the Illyrians call it, dropping its purple shadow on some distant hill or nearer valley. Yes, central Istria, with the one exception of Minho, is the loveliest country I ever saw; and I could not but apply to that, Mahomet's noble speech about Damascus —"Men can have but one Paradise; and my Paradise is fixed above."

And now two tall Venetian towers lifted themselves up on a distant hill; and passing through, for an hour more, a succession of the same scenery, we began to ascend the high hill on which Buje (pronounce the *j* as *y*) stands. Here we dined at the post-office—considering all things, a tolerable meal. The church

Buje
S. Maria.

which we had seen to the left, *S. Maria*, turned out worthless, the other, *S. Ser-*

vulus, is the ci-devant cathedral. These Istrian sees must have been very small. The *Bezirk* of Buje, (and the diocese could not have been larger) only contains 14,000 inhabitants, and twelve livings. This church is large, but entirely rebuilt—the ancient font alone remains—late in the twelfth, or early in the thirteenth century. Here it is.

Cathedral of S. Servulus.

Built into the north wall are two Roman heads in high relief, with the respective legends:—
C. VALERIVS . I. VALERIVS. A curious circular stone is inserted in the western façade; it is sculptured with Host and chalice, with the inscription—

$$\overline{\overset{\frown}{\text{CPS}}} \quad \overline{\overset{\frown}{\text{DNI}}}.$$

The tower of S. Servulus is detached, and stands on

the north side of the nave; a very common Istrian position. Of the four saints bearing the name of Servulus, who occur in the calendar, this is doubtless the martyr of Trieste, who suffered under Numerian, about A. D. 284.

In the afternoon we continued our journey through scenery, if possible, lovelier than that of the morning. Passing the little hamlets, crowded with a contented agricultural people, of Trebani and Grisignano, we crossed the River Quieto, rightly so named; eating its way, silent river, through the pleasant meadows of its own valley. Then, some two or three miles to our right, the tall Venetian towers of Montona rose on its isolated hill, the usual position of these little Istrian towns. It lies on the central Istrian road from Trieste to Mitterburg; and shortly after we entered *Visinada*

Visinada. a village lying on the eastern slope of a vine-covered hill. The church, dedicated to S. Jerome, is modern, but near its western end is this inscription, which I copied :—

C. SABE NVS
MAXIMVS
VOLTILIAE ME SE
CVNDAE VXORI
LEVCINAE ORFAE
MATRI VIVS F.E.C.
SIBI ET SVIS

There is under it a well-sculptured pitcher, and an instrument, something like a rude pair of pincers.

A little beyond Visinada, the telegraph turns to the left, on its way to Rovigno and Pola; our road follows the coast line; and, through a country of still increasing beauty, we reach Parenzo, twelve miles from Buje, about nightfall. It was the cathedral of this city which had principally led us into Istria; and, as it is certainly one of the most singular churches which primitive times have left to us, the reader will not wonder that I dwell on it at some considerable length. Few visitors, indeed, enter this deserted town—a town, however, which, in ecclesiastical interest perhaps yields only to Rome and Ravenna. Besides my own notes, I avail myself largely of Lohde's monograph, from which I have copied the frontispiece that adorns my own little volume; with its principal cathedral, some account of the ecclesiastical history of Istria will naturally mingle itself.

Parenzo stands on a peninsula; its 2,500 inhabitants entirely fill up the promontory. The *Bezirk*, of which it is the head, contains 8,249 souls, and ten parishes. The island of S. Nicolas shelters the harbour from the south-west, and renders it completely landlocked. Strabo mentions it as Παρέντιον; Pliny (Hist. Nat. iii. 23), as Parentium, or Parentum: Stephanus of Byzantium tells of its harbour. Istria, in 493, was in the hands of the Goths; in 539 the Eastern Empire reclaimed it, and it belonged to Constantinople till about 789. The Gospel was preached in Istria before the end of the first century; but the see of Parenzo is referred to the time of Theodosius the Great, S. Euphrasius being the first bishop. Under Justinian, the Istrian prelates strenuously opposed the condemnation of THE THREE CHAPTERS; and when the Aquileian schism against the V. Œcumenical council took an ecclesiastical status under the self-styled patriarch,

Paulinus, the Istrian churches followed in its lead, and not till A. D. 701 were the prelates of Illyricum, Rhœtia Secunda, and Noricum, again received into the unity of the Church.

Part of Istria, during the Lombard domination, fell into the power of those barbarians. At the destruction of their empire by Charlemagne, that part naturally attached itself to the Franks, while the other formed a portion of the Croatian Province under the Eastern Empire. In the tenth century, during the contest between Grado and Aquileia, for their patriarchal rights in Istria, Parenzo was a partizan of the latter. Later, and after many a struggle against the rising power of Venice, it, in concert with the other maritime towns, half by constraint, and half willingly, owned itself vassal of S. Mark's Lion. It was in 1192 that Parenzo became tributary to Venice; on February 15, 1267, that it was incorporated with the Venetian state, and so it remained for 530 years.

The 14th century was most calamitous in its effects. In 1354, the Genoese Admiral, Paganini Dora, appeared before the town; it was sacked and burnt, the relics of its patron saints, S. Maurus, and S. Eleutherius were carried off in triumph, and scarcely had it begun to recover from this blow, when a yet severer misfortune fell on it. The Black Death raged so violently here in 1361, that its 3,000 inhabitants were reduced to 300; and remained so till, in 1692, a Grecian colony was planted here; and later, a Slavonic population from Dalmatia poured into it. After undergoing the fortunes of the Venetian States, Istria was finally united to Austria in 1813.

Before we come to speak of the cathedral, some notice of its prelates seems necessary. We shall see from the inscription over the tabernacle that the erection of the present building is due to a certain Bishop Euphrasius, who lived during the time of a certain Pope John. Now, there is a singular difficulty in individualizing this Euphrasius.

Ughelli,* in his *Italia Sacra*, mentions Euphrasius as the first Bishop of Parentium, and fixes him at the beginning of the sixth century, though confessing that the whole matter is very uncertain. But Coletti, his editor, prints a very curious document of the year 796 in which Euphrasius " Parentinæ Ecclesiæ Præsul, curator pupillorum viduarum et orphanorum, pastor in ecclesiâ Beatæ Mariæ Virginis, et Sancti Mauri Martyris," guarantees certain privileges to his canons. These privileges are renewed by each of the succeeding bishops, 28 in number, down to Fulcherius (1208), and the Bishop Adelpert in 1219, perceiving the old document to be worn out, copies and certifies it on a new parchment. Coletti, therefore, put the Euphrasius, who was the founder of the present cathedral, as late as 796.

But two remarkable passages seem to have escaped his attention. Paullus Diaconus tells us (Hist. Longabard. III, 26) of a John, Bishop of Parenzo who in 586 followed the schismatical patriarchs of Aquileia, and was one of those four Istrian bishops whom the Patrician Smaragdus carried off by force to Ravenna. Therefore Parenzo was a see in the middle

---

* Tom. v. p. 394; Venice edition of 1721.

of the sixth century. But further, Pelagius I. (he sat from 555 to 559), thus writes to the Patrician Narses, concerning an Istrian bishop, Euphrasius:—" Quales autem sint, qui ecclesiam fugiunt, Eufrasii vos scelera, quæ amplius occulta Deus esse noluit, evidenter informant: qui in homicidio quidem nec hominis necessitudinem, nec fratris caritatem, nec sacerdotii reverentiam cogitavit."

Now the inscription on the tabernacle runs thus:

Famulus Dei Eufrasius antistes temporibus suis agens annum undecimum hunc locum condidit a fundamentis Domino Johanne beatissimo antistite Catholicæ Ecclesiæ.

We gather on the whole:

1. From Istrian tradition, that Euphrasius was first Bishop of Parenzo.

2. From the tabernacle, that Euphrasius was contemporary with *a* Pope John.

3. From Pelagius's Epistle, that in 556 or thereabouts there was *an* Euphrasius, who was an Istrian bishop; it does not say of Parenzo.

Now, which Pope John is meant by the tabernacle?

If we choose to identify Euphrasius the builder of the cathedral with Euphrasius the Istrian bishop, whom Pope Pelagius accuses of such crimes, he *might* very well have raised that edifice under John III (from 560 to 574).

But is it likely that a bishop who was engaged in an energetic schism should mention the Pope at all in his cathedral,—especially as *beatissimus* antistes: *more* especially as *Catholicæ* ecclesiæ? when he must have regarded the Patriarch of Aquileia as the true head of the Catholic church? Would he stretch

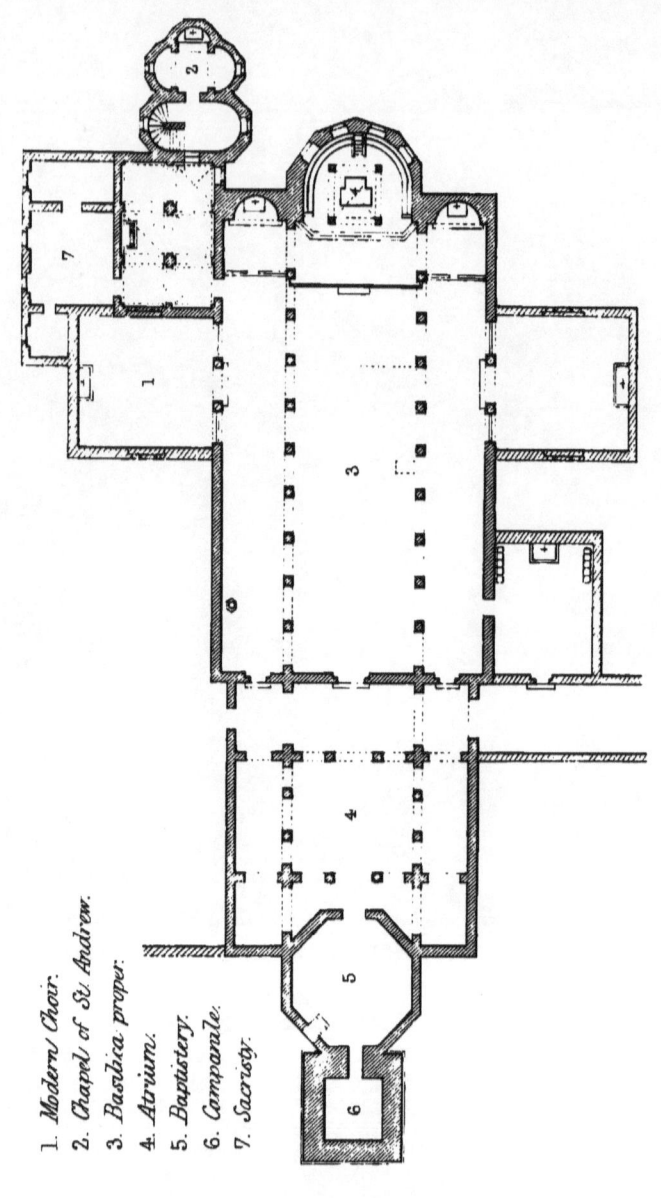

Papal prerogatives, again, when they were opposed to him ?

I cannot believe it; and let it be remembered, that there is no proof at all that this Euphrasius was Bishop of Parenzo; all we know is, that he was an Istrian prelate. But granting he was, as there was certainly another Euphrasius after him, why might there not have been another before him ? I have then little doubt that Euphrasius I, first Bishop of Parenzo, lived earlier in the sixth century, when Istria was in communion with Rome, and built this church during the pontificate of John I. (523-526). It is, therefore, of the very deepest interest. To continue our historical notice, we find in the year 961, that the cathedral was well-nigh ruined by certain barbarous Slaves; and that its then bishop, Adam, the seventeenth prelate, repaired it, and reconsecrated it. In 1233 we find Bishop Adelpert consecrating the high altar. In 1277, as we shall see, Bishop Otho erected the present Baldachin. In 1434 Citta Nova was united to the see of Parenzo by Eugenius IV; in 1451 Pope Nicholas V again separated it, and joined it to Venice. There are no further changes which we need particularise. The present Bishop Antonio Peteani is much interested in the history and restoration of his cathedral.

Now to describe the church. The ground plan with which I present the reader, will render a verbal description of it unnecessary. The apse is very noble. In the middle of the upper part, S. Mary is seated with the Divine child. On each side of her stands an angel; then to her right S. Maurus, the patron saint;

next to him, distinguished by holding a church, Euphrasius, the founder; then Claudius, the archdeacon and architect, and between these two last, a child, Euphrasius, the son of Claudius. S. Maurus, with these other personages, have their names inscribed over them. The mosaic is coarse but very effective. The Bishop Euphrasius is represented as a thin, tall man, with lean, dark face, and hollow cheeks. The underclothing of all the figures is white. Euphrasius and the Madonna have over this a reddish upper vestment. Claudius, a grey mantle with brown border; the little Euphrasius a yellow mantle, under which he appears to be holding a taper. To the left of the Madonna is an angel, and beyond him three other saints without either names or attributes: and over the head of the Mother of God, a hand extends a laurel wreath. Under the feet of these figures is, in four lines, the following inscription:—

> Hoc fuit imprimis templum quassante ruinâ
> Terribilis lapsu, nec certo robore firmum:
> Exiguo magnoque carens tum firma metallo:
> Sed meritis tantum pendebant putria tecta:
> Ut vidit subito lapsuram pondere sedem,
> Providus, et fidei fervens ardore, sacerdos
> Euphrasius sanctâ præcessit mente ruinam:
> Labentes melius redituras diruit ædes:
> Fundamenta locans erexit culmina templi.
> Quas cernis nuper vario fulgere metallo
> Perficiens cœptum decoravit munere magno:
> Ecclesiam signans vocitavit nomine Xsti:
> Congaudens opere sic felix vota peregit.

The apse is circular in the interior, hexagonal on the outside: the round-headed windows are purely Roman, a saint in Mosaic under each. The triumphal arch

has, on its broad face, medallions with the heads of female saints; on the Gospel side, six, spelt thus: Felicita, Basilissa, Eugenia, Cicilia, Agnes, Agathe; on the Epistle side, Justina, Susanna, Perpetua, Valeria, Thekla, Euphemia; while on the vertex of the arch is our LORD's monogram, also medallioned and surrounded by acanthus leaves. The ground is dark brown; the medallions of the saints, light blue, of the monograms, gold; the vestments of the saints, white, and reddish grey.

Of the nave caps, I have given two. Others represent a floriated cross, with the monogram of Euphrasius (very pretty); four vultures alternating with four jars; four swans alternating with four couple of cornucopiæ; four swans alternating with four oxen.

The baldachin, as to its general form, will be understood from the plate.

The Annunciation on the western spandrel, on a golden ground, is an exquisite design. The legend:—

> Angelus inquit Ave: quo mundus solvitur a væ.

On the side facing the altar are SS. Nebridius and (?   )

On the Epistle side, SS. Maurus and Eleutherius.

On the Gospel side, a sainted Bishop and Acolyth. The legend is:

> Tempora surgebant Christi nativa potentis
> Septem cum decies, septem cum mille ducentis,
> Virginis absque pare cum sacræ sedulus aræ
> Hoc opus ex voto perfecit episcopus Oto,
> Perpetuando pia, laudes tibi, Virgo Maria.
> Hoc quicunque legis, dic, O Virguncula munda,
> Cui nec prima fuit, nec succes [sura] secunda,

> Et tu Sancte Dei Martyr celeberrime Maure,
> Pro nobis Christi vox intercedat in aure:
> Ut divinus amor lustret præcordia turbæ,
> Et dulcis pacis concordia crescet in urbe.
> Ut tandem tota cordis rubigine lota,
> Et prorsus demptis tenebris de lumine mentis,
> Cum jam succident vitalia stamina Parcæ,
> Nos miserante Deo cœli salvemur in Arce.   Amen.

On the very curious altar hanging, we have the following, in golden letters, on a darkened ground:

> Si capitur digne capientem servat ab igne:
> Qui rodit, mandit, cor, os, et guttura tangit:
> Intestina tamen non tangit nobile stamen,
> Esca salutaris quæ sacris ponitur aris;
> Si male sumatur, sumenti pæna paratur.

I must not forget to mention the remarkably fine renaissance frontal of silver gilt, which this altar possesses.

In the chapel of S. Andrew, at the south east, two very curious things are preserved. The one, the tabernacle, coeval with the Cathedral, of which I am bound to give a drawing. The other, the Sarcophagus, prepared as a shrine for SS. Maurus and Eleutherius; it is of fine grey marble, and the inscription, composed by Bishop Paganus in 1247, runs thus:

✝ ANN. DNI. MILLO. DUCT. XLVII. INDICT. V RESIDENTE. DNO PAGANO.
ET JONE. ARCHIPRO. NECNON. TOMA. DIAC. ET. OTONE. SUBD. TESAURAR.
QUI. AD. HONOREM. DEI. ET. SCOR. MART. MAVRI. ET. ELEV-THERII FECER.
FIERI. HOC. OP. MAURE. PARENTINOS. CONSERVA. INCOLUMES. AMEN.

It was again restored by Bishop Aloysio Tasso (1500—1516) in 1508; as this additional inscription shows:

ALOV. TAS. EPI. PAR. NAT. BERGO. CURA. INSTAVRATUM.
AN.M.D.VIII.

I could dwell longer on this most interesting church with great pleasure, but I must remember that my work is a Tour in Dalmatia, not a history of Parenzo. I have only to add, that the great north transept, seen, as a modern addition in the plan, is the present choir. Vespers were said very well, while I was studying the church.

I find *S. Maria*, Parenzo, set down as of interest. But I have no description of it, and imagine it, therefore, to be a modern church.

We might have continued our route by land to Pola; but, so far as I could learn, no object of particular interest lies between the two cities; and as we had still some arrangements to make for our Dalmatian Tour, we slept one night at Parenzo, and then returned by steamer to Trieste. Here we remained two days. On a Saturday, having arranged our communications with the Consul, we again left Trieste, at six in the morning, by the Kaiserinn Elizabeth (I think) a very comfortable boat. Calling at Pirano and Rovigno, we coasted along Istria all day, and were astonished how flat from the sea that glorious country looks. In the afternoon we passed the interesting little Greek colony of Peroi; and soon after entered the narrow strait between the island Buoni and Fasani. Here the scenery, with green fertile coast to the left, and innumerable islets to the right,—becomes very picturesque; and presently, rounding Cape de Sauci, we go—moment never to be forgotten—into Pola harbour.

We pass the little island of S. Catherine, whose

church we are presently to visit: but the ground-plan

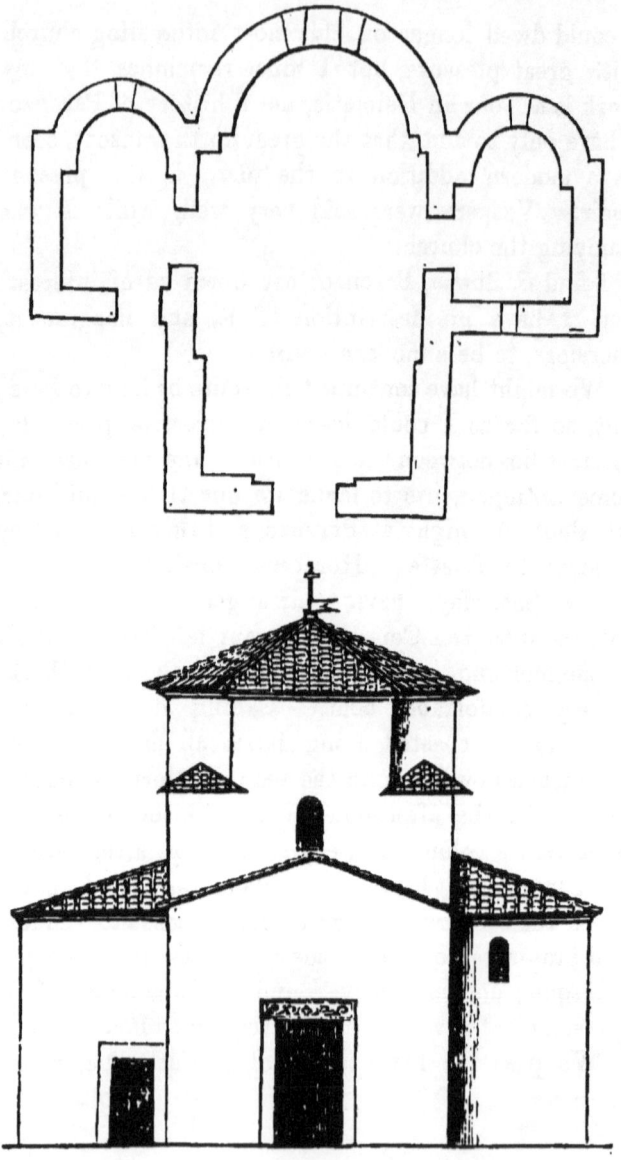

and western façade will give the reader a sufficient idea of it. It is possibly of the sixth century.

Sir Humphry Davy thought Pola harbour one of the most glorious views in the world. And marvellously beautiful it is. To our left rose the three tiers of the amphitheatre, of snow-white marble, but then reflecting the redness of a cloudless May evening. White cottage and tall spire gleamed here and there from the thick foliage of the Istrian hills. The peasant drove his oxen—it was Saturday evening—to the pastures; the vesper bells rang out from the Cathedral; the Adriatic was an unbroken sheet of gold; the "Cheerily, men! oh, cheerily!" came from an English vessel weighing anchor.

First to the amphitheatre. As I have said, it is of white marble, its long axis parallel to the sea; the three rows of arches are perfect everywhere, except in the (quasi) last, where the ground rises, and there are two only. The lowest and second row, of circular heads; the upper, square.

Every single feature is beautifully clear; the doors; the trapdoor-holes above; the canal; the holes for the awning poles; in several stones the width allowed to each spectator is marked by a boldly-cut line. The architectural curiosity of the amphitheatre consists in the four square towers, at four cardinal points, projecting from the ellipse, and supposed to have been the Vomitories. The larger axis is 436, the shorter, 346 feet in length; it is calculated that 18,000 spectators could find sitting room. The wall, when perfect, was 97 feet high. Each of the stories contains 72 arches.

But details are swallowed up in the one feeling that many and many a martyr has stood on the same holy ground; and that where I now, note-book in hand, gaze around, and observe the loveliness of the deep blue sky, as seen through the ruined marble arch, members of the same church have stood, waiting the spring of the beast that was to send them to glory.

> Carcerati, trucidati,
>   Tormentorum genera,
> Igne læsi, ferro cæsi,
>   Pertulerunt plurima.
> Dum sic torti cedunt morti
>   Carnis per interitum,
> Ut electi sunt adepti
>   Beatorum præmium.
> Ergo facti cohæredes
>   Christi in cœlestibus,
> Apud eum vota nostra
>   Promovete precibus;
> Ut post finem hujus vitæ,
>   Et post transitoria,
> Mereamur in perenni
>   Exultare Patriâ!

We turned sorrowfully away, though to a cathedral of marvellous interest.

Pola Cathedral. The cathedral is as follows:

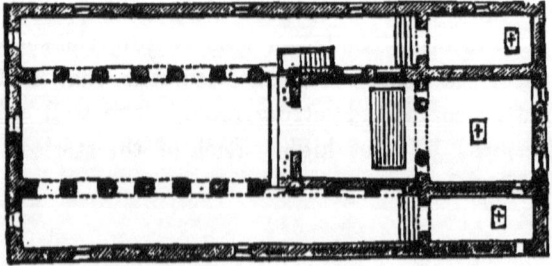

The chief peculiarity is its square east end. Remarkable as the building is, it does not afford any extended ground for description. In the south wall is this inscription:—

   AN. INCARNAT. DNI. DCCCLVII.
   IND. V. REGNE. LVDOVICO. IMP. AVGVSTO
   IN. ITALIA. HANDEGIS. HVJVS. ECCLESIE.

The rest is lost.

I may observe that though we made diligent inquiries in this city, now numbering some 4,000 inhabitants, and on account of the docks which Austria is here forming, an important place, we could procure no description or engraving of the cathedral or amphitheatre! Why Murray's *Hand Book* gives the date of the cathedral as of the fifteenth century I cannot imagine.

The ascent to the choir is by nine steps. The soleas is of three, the nave proper of seven bays—in all ten. The triumphal arch is very broad : its piers are circular, on square base, and with square flowered caps. The easternmost three piers, that is those in the soleas, have square stilted base, circular shaft, square flowered cap. The easternmost arch is, on both sides, pointed. The piers in the nave proper are the same, except that the bases are not stilted. The material is of coarse grey Istrian marble. The aisle windows, three in each side, seem to have been recast to their present form, trefoiled lancets, in the thirteenth century. The clerestory consists of semi-circular windows. There is a detached western tower, but it is modernised.

On one side of the market place are two adjacent

temples. That on your left, as you stand facing them, was dedicated to *Augustus* and *Rome*; it is small but very perfect; the Corinthian portico is much admired by antiquaries. The place is now a museum. The other is the *Temple of Diana*. It has now an elegant, though late Venetian front, having been the palace of the governor. The façade has four circular headed arches, circular base, circular shaft, square caps. I suppose it to be late in the thirteenth century, an imitation of Romanesque. I copied, as well as waning light would let me, the following inscription:

> . . . at Patavi Vitrei cognominis hæres,
> . patriæ præses Bartholomæus erat.
> A partu Mariæ lustris revoluta ducentis
> Per sexagenum ceperat ire dies :
> Cum fabricata fuit domus hæc veneranda duorum,
> Consilii sedes, judiciique locus :
> Hæc duo si fuerint sensato preta (?) ministro,
> Vix erit ut populum deseret alma quies.
> Unanimes igitur foveat concordia cives,
> . . . . sanum viscere sæva caput.

Pola Franciscan Convent.

The most lovely ecclesiastical building in Pola (and probably in Istria) is the late *Franciscan Convent*, now a military magazine. With great trouble, both moral and physical, I got into the church; but that is so blocked up by alterations, and filled with military equipments that we could not form any clear general idea of it. There is an excellent quadrangle. On the north side of the nave, is a double row of apertures, perhaps of the fifteenth century—the lower, circular headed semi-classical arches—the upper, elegant octagonal shafts, bevelled into square base and cap, and supporting the wooden eaves, without any arch.

The east side contains one of the most elegant First-pointed doors, between two windows, that I ever saw. The mouldings of the door are very elaborate. The windows of two trefoiled lights, divided by a lovely shaft, daintily pierced with a little trefoil on its head. You enter the church towards the south end of the western side of the cloister. To your left is a dedication cross of this shape. It consists chiefly of chancel and nave, and must have been very solemn. Chancel of one bay; simple cross vaulting; the vaulting shafts massy and gloomy. At the east end are two adjacent trefoiled lights, clearly by the same hand as those in the cathedral. The nave, if ever it were vaulted, which I doubt, is now open to the roof.  There is a small north chapel to choir. At the south end of the building, which commands a glorious view over the bay, is a most delicious Middle-pointed door of eight orders, twisted and twined in every conceiveable form, a most remarkable example of the poetry of stone. Over this is an eight-foiled rose. I would advise any architect who finds himself with an hour or two in Pola (some of the steamers stop only that time), to make the Franciscan Convent, rather than anything else, and in that convent, this door and window, his object.

Δύσετο τ' ἠέλιος · σκιόωντο τε πᾶσαι ἀγυιάι.

We walked back to our inn, a small filthy pothouse. The people were very civil, but charged exorbitantly. Here I first saw, and vainly tried to eat, that vilest of meats, a boiled cuttle fish. Its large, lanky, leathery, clammy, arms, in being cut up, gave me the impression of hacking away at tough worms.

Late at night we went on board the steamer, which, on its way to Fiume, was to drop us, next morning, at Malinski in Veglia. Quite tired out with the week's hard work, I turned in to my very comfortable berth with singular satisfaction, and have an indistinct impression of being woke by the silence of the paddles in the middle of the night, and congratulating myself that we were in Cherso harbour, one of our calling places, and that, by consequence, I had some hours of repose yet.

Chapter VI.

VEGLIA; OSSERO; AND TO ZARA.

MAP OF VEGLIA AND PLAUNICH.

I NEVER remember a more peaceful Sunday morning than that which broke over us in the Quarnero. To the right, as our vessel stood south-eastwards, rose the woody peaks of Cherso in all their green beauty; an unclouded sun sleeping on their glorious masses of foliage, backed by the wild heights of Istria, on some of whose serrated peaks and crags the snow still hung. Immediately in front of us was the flatter island of Veglia, of a fainter verdure, and spotted here and there by the purple shadows of four playful clouds. Before, towered the vast mountain range of Croatia; great Vellebitchi, princely Marzuran, the gentler chain of the Kapella, and monarch of all, Kleck, sparkling in its deep snows. Between Cherso and Veglia, faint in the distance, lay the grey shadow of Plaunich. How lovely it was, that calm shallow sea—the sun-rays piercing it in a thousand golden or beryl paths, and casting quivering spangles and drops of light on the golden sand,—or the rock where the purple sea-anemone spread its blossoms, and the sea-rose its broader leaves. Now and then the breeze, freshening, brought the sound of church bells, or the music of nightingales from sweet Cherso; now and then, a distant wave flashed into snow on some black rock,—or a distant vessel, tacking, glanced like a white sea bird.

It was Rogation Sunday. And now I began to make out a spire or two on the nearing coast of Veglia: and to see groups of peasants wending their slow way to mass from the beach-cottage, or the vine-concealed hut. And so we cast anchor in the little bay of Malinski. The post-master, Lloyd's agent, and general factotum for that part of the island, came off in a boat: and with the hearty Austrian wish of *Glückliche Reise* from our captain, and from our late fellow-passengers, we pulled towards the village-quay, and the steamer stood northward for Fiume.

Anxious to see all I could of the Glagolita rite, I

had resolved to walk round the western coast of the island, where no carriage can penetrate. My companion preferred the easier conveyance of a two-horse car along the one Veglian road; and, as my way at first was the same as his, we started together. I should have thought that, as only one road is carriageable, our driver could not have missed his way; but Lloyd's officer, awe-struck with the official paper I produced, actually paid a man to run before us and prevent all possibility of error.

The Bay of Malinski is a pretty piece of scenery; vineyards that slope down to the white pebbly beach, dog-roses that skirt the country road; olives and apple trees occupying vantage places amidst the rocky soil; and, as the road, after skirting the sea-shore, proceeds towards the hills, wheat and barley fields, each enclosed by its rude stone wall. About a mile from the quay, stands the new church, for Malinski was, till lately, in the parish of Dobasnizza. As we walked up to it, we were passed by the sexton, and I had the satisfaction of learning that one of my objects was fulfilled. "Is the service in Latin in this church?" "No," was the reply; "it is said here in Croatian—or, I ought rather to say, in Illyrian." The building itself is worthless, though clean and roomy: chancel and nave—the altar standing between the two. In the choir, I for the first time saw Glagolita books. There were two ambones, *used* too, as the sexton said.

Striking westwards, a quarter of a mile brought me to the chapel of *S. Antonio*. It is very small; circular apse, nave, western loggia— a rude Romanesque building. The apse, wagon-vaulted.

S. Antonio.

The nave-roof open, of low pitch, painted in the fourteenth or fifteenth century, with a checkie pattern; white, grey, and blue; one small Romanesque light on each side. There is a cinquecento chrismatory. The porch, a low wall, with red and white marble shafts that support the roof—old men there waiting for mass, to commence in half an hour. Here I first made trial of my little stock of Slavonic; which, derived from the ancient language only, must have had a ludicrously archaic effect to my auditors. However, it served as a medium of communication, and a cheerful, contented pastoral people they seemed. Veglia is a perfect labyrinth of cross paths. Rock, rock, rock, stone, stone, stone, everywhere; deep rocky lanes, broad stony moors; forests and forests of one low bright-leaved bush; the turf, such as it is, painted with orchises, cowslips, and primroses. Walking so fatiguing I never remember; every step has to be picked—sharp rocks, round rocks, square rocks—sharp stones, square stones, round stones; fixed rocks, moving rocks, and fixed stones, moving stones, mile after mile. The country is pretty enough: now heathy hills, now the bush-forest; sometimes a wheat field, to be measured by feet, or rather inches.

How often was I reminded of the parable in Isaiah, of the "vineyard on a very fruitful hill," where the lord "fenced it, and gathered out the stones thereof!" The stones, here so gathered out, form the wall of the field—a wall not rarely as thick as the field is broad. And what play-grounds for lizards those walls are! How their green and gold contrasts with the white spar, or the grey lichen! And what pretty little beasts they are! Often and often have I watched them turn their heads this way and that way, for the least sound of danger, and then securely basking in the fierce and reflected sun-ray. In the hollow of the crescent-shaped wall, I passed one herd of cattle, which were diligently turning over the stones for the scant short herbage below them,—when a black serpent, at least four feet long, darted across my path. So I passed westward and upwards, till I again caught a view of the sea—the narrow blue strait. Mount Lyss, in Cherso, directly opposite—the white spire of Predoschizza at its foot: Mount Goly, in Istria, towering behind both. And, at the same time, I caught sight of the tall tower of my own immediate goal, *Poglizza*.

The church was worthless; a large pseudo-classical white building; altar at west end of choir: but I was in time for a Glagolita mass. The epistle and gospel were read, not from the Missal, but from the *Pistole i Evangelja*, of which I have already spoken. It was, I confess, with singular interest that I heard the *Sctènje knighè Blàxenòga Jakova Aposctolà* given out. Here also were two ambones, both used: only in the gospel, the acolyth did not ascend with the taper, but stood in front and below the Priest. The congregation, of some 300, were very devout; men on the north, women on the south, side; the married of both sexes, east; the unmarried, west. The Priest, before the creed, and still in the ambo, made a short address with reference to the Rogation Processions, and ending with a few words on the efficacy of prayer. I should observe, that neither in this church, nor

Poglizza.

anywhere on the island, did I find the slightest sign of, or allusion to, the month of Mary. Mass ended, the worthy Incumbent invited me to share a bottle of Cyprus wine. I asked him how far the people understood the Illyric office? a question to which I was anxious to have a clear answer. "Enough," he said, "to carry away the general meaning of a passage. But stay," he continued, "did you ever read Rabelais in the original?" "Yes." "Well, about as well as a French peasant could understand that dialect, so do these the office." The reader will hereafter see both more, and less, favourable accounts of the same matter. My worthy host preached on the principal festivals, usually translating or adapting Segneri: he seemed pleased when I told him that an English Priest had translated the more striking sermons of that great preacher.

S. Fosca. Leaving Poglizza, my way was to *S. Fosca*, nearer the Strait; a church nearly the fac-simile of *S. Antonio*. But here, much hidden by lime-cast, I made out the inscription:—

. . . . ed. April, consecrat. per manus . . . ano millesimo nongessimo tertio.

I should have, without more than internal evidence, fixed the erection of the church to 1100. One cannot but remember, with reference to the somewhat rare dedication, the church of *S. Fosca* at Torcello; earlier even than this. S. Fosca, or Fusca, was a Ravennate Martyr, in the persecution of Diocletian.

From this point, through a tangled bush wilderness, and groping my way through a labyrinth of paths, I at length saw, from the brow of a hill, and far below me, the silver line of the Jesero-See,—Veglia's one lake. Entering *the* road close to it, I soon reached the heights that lie above the capital. Veglia stands well at the head of a little bay,—a quaint, mediæval, fortified town,—with a chapel, such an one as we should in Portugal call an *ermida*, near each gate. These chapels have their nave open on three sides; the roof usually lean-to, and supported by marble shafts, without arches, rising from a wall three feet or three feet six inches high. Veglia is a city of narrow streets; of gardens, terraced steeply up the abrupt hill-banks; vine corridors and arbors running along the top of rough-cast walls; while every now and then you meet a portly, gentlemanly-looking Canon, with his crimson collars and stockings, the Church, in these parts, being by no means in an impoverished condition. There is a tolerable inn; not more dirty nor vermin-haunted than usual, and the people are civil.

Now for the *Cathedral*. The see of Veglia contains that island, Cherso, and Plaunich; that of Arbe; and three parishes in the island of Pago. It is in the metropolitan province of Gorz. In Veglia, every parish church and chapel—the cathedral, which is also parochial, alone excepted—is, as I have said, of the Glagolita Rite; thirteen in all, with a population of 15,283 souls. Besides this, that rite is employed in the convent of the third Illyrian Order of S. Francis at Veglia; in that of S. Maria Capo; in that of Dobasnizza; and in that of Valle de S. Martino, in Cherso. In the case of mixed marriages between a Glagolitic and Latin Catholic, the children follow the rite of the father; but there is an exception in favour of the eldest daughter of a Glagolitic family. Though she marry a Latin, she and her husband are at liberty, at their marriage, to choose the rite to which she and her children will belong; and, becoming a widow, she is again permitted to make her own choice.

Veglia
S. Mark.
The *Cathedral* is of Romanesque date, and rather valuable. It consists of choir, soleas, nave; aisles to all; chapels to north aisle; western tower and narthex, as hereafter to be described. The choir, which contains a circular apse and two bays, is thoroughly and hopelessly modernised. The soleas has two bays, and is divided both from choir and nave by low marble cinque-cento rails. Of the same date are the ambones on its western side. The nave has seven bays; piers, mostly circular, some few octagonal; square Corinthianising capitals, well worked in flowers or beasts; bases, octagonal or circular, as the pier. The chapels are later. The first, entered by an elaborately worked pointed arch; shaft with white marble cap, base octagonal; it has three small lancets : the second may be original; arch, circular, and, I believe,'Romanesque : the third, of First-pointed details, is very small. The font, at the west end of the nave, an octagonal block slightly tapering from the upper part to the base. The west end is very singular. Imagine a triapsidal church, with western tower, set down at right angles to the west end of the Cathedral, so that its east end should point south,

and you have an idea of this strange adoption. The whole is under one vast flattish roof, gabled, of course, north and south. What may be called the north aisle of our supposed erection is now turned into a passage, between it and the cathedral. The central apse, circular, is a noble bit of Romanesque; a nebuly moulding running round the cornice. The *southern* apse is smaller, but in other respects the same; there are no lights. The north end of this strange adoption is partly ruinous, partly built against; but the tower is remarkable. Very lofty, it has three stages, and ends in a wretched cupola; there is a great Romanesque belfry light north, and another west. An inscription, very difficult to decipher, states that it was restored *imperante Aloysio Mocenigo duce Venetiarum.* Veglia was an independent state till ceded to Venice in 1481. There can be no doubt that the Cathedral was the church erected in 1133, as a thanksgiving for a great victory over Corsairs; and dedicated to S. Mark, in acknowledgment of the assistance rendered by the Venetian Republic. The building well deserves the attention of ecclesiologists; but is in the most miserable state of restoration possible. Piers and arches are "ornamented" with crimson and yellow frippery; the stalls, wretched; filth and squalor everywhere. This ought not to be, for the bishop has a residence in the town, and the chapter is well off, and commands great respect.

I proceed to the other churches:

That of the *Franciscans*, in the upper part of the city, is of the latter part of the twelfth century. Chancel, with square

Veglia
S. Francisco.

east end, long nave without aisles, tower south of chancel. The altar stands under the chancel arch; the choir, as always here, being behind. At the east end, two lancets: south of chancel, one: plain cross vaulting. The nave is very plain; no lights on its north side; on its south, are trefoiled lancets, which reminded me of Pola. There is a modern gallery at the west end, in which the office is said; it is the Glagolita. Over the door, otherwise plain, is the Lion of Venice, which must be a later addition. The tower is lofty and plain; of five stages. The belfry windows are double, circular headed; the dividing shaft square, with flowered caps. In this church I heard Glagolita Tierce and Sexts. In the cathedral, the vespers were very well and congregationally sung. There was a full assembly of canons, and the bishop was in his place. It was a very excellent example of a town, Sunday-afternoon, service.

Veglia
S. Maria.
S. Maria stands on the opposite side of the road, and close to S. Francisco. The position of the respective towers — here at the west end, there near the east — gives an odd effect. Apsidal choir, nave, two aisles, western tower. It is of the twelfth century. The ritual choir is behind the altar. The apse is circular; one eastern lancet. The nave has five bays; the arches are round; the piers circular, the caps, square and Corinthianizing; the windows are of that stable kind, which we have already had occasion to notice. The tower also forms the porch. Of two stages, it has, in the belfry, two circular headed lights. Between the two a pilaster buttress.

There is also a Conventual church of *Clarissines*, but it has unfortunately been rebuilt. *Clarissine Church.*

In the afternoon we paid a visit to the Island of *Zoccolante*, which belongs to the third Illyrian order of S. Francis. Embarking, therefore, at the primitive little quay of Veglia we rowed across the bay in an easterly direction, till we had doubled the promontory of S. Maria. Then there opened out a pretty bay; the whole village of Ponte, and its Venetian tower, couching below the high eastern down; detached and at some little distance from the town, the country residence of the bishop. In the very midst of the bay, a little thickly-wooded island, with a tower rising above the limes and oaks and cypresses of the conventual grounds. A tiny pier formed the landing place; beyond this was a boat-house; *Zoccolante.* and by the side of the latter, under the tall limes, sat three Brothers, looking out on the wide unruffled bay, spotted here and there by the purple shadow of a passing cloud. As our boat touched the shore, they came forward and received us most courteously; and, on entering the trellised corridor that leads from the boat-house to the porch, we were welcomed by the venerable head of the convent—an old man who might have sat to Fra Angelico for one of his saintly figures. The community consists of five priests, two clerks, three brothers, and two servitors. The church was unfortunately "rebuilt" in 1721. It is of the usual arrangement. Choir, with a square east-end, behind the altar. Over the latter is a very large and tolerable picture of the Joys of Paradise. The cloisters, if not picturesque, are convenient,—roses, syringas, and daffodils lighted up the quadrangle, while an old laburnum flung its golden blossoms against the grey arch of the entrance door. The Illyrian marbles both of cloister and church are exquisitely grained, and worked with admirable care. The library is poor. I saw there the *Editio Princeps* of Silius Italicus, 1481,—and Lucan, 1472. We then went into the prior's sitting-room, and were regaled with the vintage of an estate belonging to the House at Ponte; a good wine, somewhat resembling red Voslauer. The conversation turned on the present position of the Pope, and on the pamphlet, which was lying on the table, *Le Pape et l'Empereur*. While execrating Victor Emmanuel, and still more Cavour, the good fathers were not ultramontane. They did not like the "novelty" of the Month of Mary; and, from the way in which they declined, when I alluded to it, the subject of the Immaculate Conception, I gathered that they belong to that minority —in Austria a large minority—which was opposed to the promulgation of the new dogma. One of them pointed out, in a volume of Latin poetry, called *Amores Mariani*, written by Melchior Guthwirth, a Jesuit, and published at Linz, in 1690, what he called a neat rejoinder to some of the usual arguments against the novel doctrine. The reader may not be displeased to see a specimen of this polemical ratiocination in elegiacs. The worthy prior having made me a present of the book, I quote it from that :

> Acriter occlamant : *in Adam peccavimus omnes* :
> Ergo labe carens esse Maria nequit.
> Omnibus est data lex, bene magnus Apostolus inquit :

Supra omnes, non *ex* omnibus illa fuit.
Cur aliquos fallat, quod vox ibi ponitur *omnis*?
Non omnes vox hæc *omnis* utique legat.
Omnis homo mendax. An, homo quod et ipsa Maria,
Sic etiam mendax esset habenda tibi?
Nonne reformidat durum reverentia dictum?
A Dominâ longe quam dolus omnis erat!
Quod *caro* justitiæ leges corruperit *omnis*,
Ultrici mundum perdidit imbre Deus:
Et tamen hic *omnes* cum corrupisse feruntur,
Inter eos purâ mente Noemus erat.

I found them acquainted with the admirable and crushing articles which appeared in the "Observateur Catholique,"—till stopped by the civil authority—on the Bishop of Bruges's work in defence of the bull *Ineffabilis*. In speaking of the Glagolita, they affirmed it to be the modern hearth-language of the common people. (It must be remembered that they have no practical acquaintance with its employment, as this is a Latin convent.) We both noticed the apparent dislike with which they spoke of its permissive use: just as I remember, some years ago, to have heard the Præmonstratensians of Strahov express their disapprobation of the Tcheck as employed in the Theinkirche at Prague.

Bidding a farewell to our hosts, we were landed at the nearest point of the shore; and thence strolled over the hills, a forty minutes' walk, into Veglia. The Rosary was being said with great energy by a large congregation in S. Maria, as we passed.

On the following morning we started on foot for Besca Nuova, at the south-eastern extremity of the island, intending there to meet the steamer from the south, and to make our way by it to Zengh. A sumpter horse, under the charge of Giuseppe Dundich, was to follow. Our path first skirted the bay of Zoccolante—then began to rise—and gave us a precipitous ascent of an hour and a half. In the meantime, distant growlings of thunder began to echo among the Croatian mountains—the clouds gathered and blackened—and when we came out on the high backbone of the island, we were drenched through and through. Here, quite exhausted with thirst, I knelt down to drink out of a rocky pool; and shutting my eyes, as one naturally does when they are close to the water, I felt something move across my lips. Looking to see what it was, I beheld a monstrous black snake making his way to a cleft in the adjacent rock; and, fancying his presence had not improved the taste of the water, I discontinued my draught. The descent on the other side was singularly beautiful. The gorge itself, with the clear bright green Fiumera dashing down it; still more so, the bay of Besca Nuova, with the Island of Pervicchio immediately in front, and the savage heights of Ponte Scoglia to our right.

Though the day was again fine, there were still ominous mutterings in the Croatian range, of which we were better to understand the meaning before the evening. We passed *Besca Valle*, a new white church, with a Venetian tower, as well as several roadside ermidas, and in about five hours reached the sea-port village of *Besca Nuova*. Streets and alleys so narrow that two men can scarcely pass; so foul, that the stenches of centuries seem there imprisoned; and yet, the very feet of the filthy vermin-

Besca Valle.

tenanted houses are washed by the pure green waves of the lovely bay. The steamer made its appearance, but our sumpter horse had not arrived; and very unwillingly we were forced to let it go without us. In half an hour the missing party came up, with a history of accidents—how the wretched beast had fallen three times—how the straps broke and our luggage rolled down the rocks. We hired a boat with four oars, and started for Zengh. But now the wind rose, and I was quite surprised to see how soon it lashed the Quarnerulo, like a glass all the morning, into fury. We rounded Ponte Luka, the south-eastern extremity of the island; then, first whispers, then ominous looks and expressions, and at last the men said we must put about at once, and I heard the word, the dread of Adriatic sailors—Bora. They carried every stitch of canvas; for the sea by this time was very high, the great, hungry, green waves running after us: and, as the boat would not sail near the wind, there was considerable risk of our going ashore on Ponte Luka. The sky was pitch black, the lightning almost incessant, and the thunder bellowed and roared, echoed from Veglia to Pervicchio, and from Pervicchio to Veglia. When we came within a quarter of a mile of the rock, our men gave themselves up to their Litanies, leaving the sails to our care. Nearer we came, and nearer, to the great black point, on which, through the scud of rain, we could see the foam of the breakers dashed high into the air. For a few minutes our chance seemed very doubtful; but, providentially, the wind fell off two or three points, and like a racehorse we flew round the headland, about two boats' lengths

Besca Nuova.

from it. Then the gabbling of voices was indescribable as different plans were discussed. To get back to Besca Nuova was impossible, it lying too near the wind, and the sea running too high for oars. Some were for running to Cherso, others to Smerzo, or Kruskizza; but the nearest of these little harbours was 30 miles off. At last, after hearing all sides, I determined for Veglia—I mean the city. But running under the Scoglio Gagli—it looked so savagely gloomy on that wild night—the wind again shifted, and Veglia became an impossibility. Then the men proposed Besca Vecchia; where, they said, the priest would give us lodging; and by dint of great exertion we made our way into a little creek at the end of the village about nine o'clock, drenched and exhausted. It was pitch dark; we scrambled along a cliff-path, and in half an hour were knocking at the door of a little white house, close to the church, and like it, overhanging the cliff. The priest was going to bed; he welcomed us most kindly, congratulated us on our escape, offered us all he had—bread and coffee, and, quite beyond our expectation, a bed. But such a state of filth, grease, vermin, and everything loathsome, I never before saw; the more inexcusable since our host was very well off, and a considerable landed proprietor. He told us that he had the Rogation Procession to lead at 2·30 A. M., but that he reckoned on seeing us at breakfast. Most glad were we to throw ourselves on the bed, let it be what it might, and scarcely were we disturbed by the heavy clang of the bells first, and then the hymns, as the village procession wound away towards the hills. At seven we were aroused with the intelligence that it was a bright day, the sea calm, and the boat moored under the cliff. Breakfast, and a very grateful farewell to our host, and we embarked again; sailed pleasantly past Zoccolante, and in two hours reached Veglia.

In the afternoon, the steamer arrived from Fiume, bound to Lussingrande in the island of Ossero. As we pursued our voyage through the Quarnerulo, the sea gleamed with all the hues of a peacock's neck; to our right, the great Monte Maggiore, in Istria, towered above the hills of Cherso; to our left, the snow-capped peaks of Croatia glowed in that heavenly pink which barely seems to belong to this world. Soon, black Point Colnach, the southern extremity of Cherso, rose close to us; seamed and scarred rocks, twisted and contorted as if by magic; while a few tall pines stood out in strong relief against the golden western sky. The goat bell rang from the little Island of Palaziol, as the long white wave rippled on its shore; and then to our right came into view the green, but feverish island of Ossero. Night fell around us as we began to run along its eastern coast, and about ten we cast anchor in the harbour of Lussingrande. We had the Captain's leave to sleep on board, contrary, by the way, to the Company's usual custom.

I have not yet mentioned the printed regulations for the behaviour of passengers, which read well enough in the stilted solemnity of the Greek. They are appealed to, ὡς ἄνθρωποι καλῶς ἀνατεθράμμενοι, to behave well εἰς τὸ φῦλον (γένος) an odd double expression; either phrase to be translated—*the sex*. And in the saloon it is forbidden να καπνίζῃ τις καπνόν· and especially for gentlemen εἰσέρχεσθαι εἰς τὰς καμέρας τῶν Κυρίων (δεσποίνων).

At four next morning, I went on deck, and found that we were lying in a small bay, surrounded by an amphitheatre of vineyards, and spotted with a few white houses to our right. This was Lussingrande, a very insignificant place. We pulled round the point of the bay, to the right, to get *pratique*, and after some difficulty, were graciously allowed to continue our voyage. Rowing along the coast for a mile further, we again landed, and, mounting a steep hill, found that we had crossed the island of Ossero; here not more than three-quarters of a mile broad. Its western side is indented, like its eastern, by a bay; but Lussin-piccolo is a very important place; next to Fiume, the most important in Croatia. The *Cathedral* stands high on the hill to your right, as you descend to the town; on that to the left are most of the consular residences. The best houses stand round the quay; the bay is admirable as a harbour, and frequented by steamers from Trieste. The island Ossero is about eighteen miles long, and nowhere more than two, seldom than one, broad. To the north-east, it is separated from Cherso by a very narrow strait, the Viaia. It contains five villages; Neresne to the north; then S. Giacomo; then Chiunschi; then the capital; last of all, Lussingrande. It forms a deanery in the diocese of Parenzo-Pola, but has no Glagolita parish.

Ossero, which gives the island its name, is, oddly enough, a village in Cherso, just opposite to the island called from it. In the north, Mount Ossero; in the south, Mount Calvario, are fine objects; but the island is, generally speaking, unhealthy.

Lussinpiccolo is rather an imposing place; the population amounts to 7,000. The steamer by which we were to continue our voyage, was already in the harbour; but was not to start for three hours. After breakfasting at a decent coffee house on the quay, I bent my way, up a series of steps with broad landing places between each staircase, to the platform on which the *Cathedral*—it has long ceased to be so—stands. A large, spacious, modern church, with ambones; the marbles very beautiful. The tower, as usual, to the north of the nave. There was at 6·30 A.M., a fair congregation; mass going on at a side altar.

Cathedral.

We went on board the steamer, and soon saw a very pretty sight. The little battery fired a single cannon; forthwith, the bells of the Cathedral clanged out, answered by a perfect storm of bell-music from chapels in the town. Presently, over the quay at the lower end of the Cathedral staircase, gleamed a silver cross; then came acolytes, deacons, priests, —the Dean of Lussin,— girls' schools, boys' schools. And presently rose the sounds, so lusciously sweet to hear, so rude and barbarous in their western clothing:

>Bij dan nami, rodyen nami
>   Od Dieyiççœ neoçqyargnenœ,
>Sfeta Zakon besiedami
>   Vierhiem prossu;—i uçknenœ
>Potaynostiy' doyarscio
>Redom cudmem, kakoy'htio:

i.e. the *Nobis datus, nobis natus* of S. Thomas's great hymn.

Priests, Benedictines, Franciscans of the third Illyrian Order, Bridgettines, schools, and crowd,—they all poured into a chapel on the quay, which it seemed marvellous could contain so many; and they had not finished the *Lauda Sion Salvatorem*—I knew it by its melody—when our paddles ploughed up the quiet bay, and we stood out to sea.

Sansego.
The little island of *Sansego*, green and fertile, lay to our right. The church seems of Flamboyant date; the windows worthless; but the south door good. The river-like passage between the southern part of Ossero to the left, and the island of S. Pietro de Nembo to the right; again, between the latter and Asinaria, is very lovely; dark, jutting rocks, at the foot of which the blue Quarnero heaves and laughs: pines arching themselves half-down the precipice; crag-hawks wheeling and screaming for joy round the peaks; dappled goats bounding from rock to rock; the goat-herd's pipe, scrannel enough, I dare say in itself, coming mellowed by the distance.

And now the sea becomes spotted with islands. Straight a-head is Selve; we shall land there presently; to the left is Ulbe. Far before us, the clustering Dalmatian groups seem to be solid land: patience, and they will open out. In the meantime, we are running along flat, dull Selve. "*Stop her!*—and who is for shore?" "Captain Knezevitch, is there time to go ashore?" "I suppose I must make it for you; there,—that is the way to the church."

Selve is our first Dalmatian land. It forms the most important deanery in the diocese of Zara. Itself is Latin, but most of its dependent parishes are Glagolita; the old rite hangs about the islands longer than in the mainland. The church consists of square chancel, nave, aisles to the latter; Venetian tower, south of nave. Choir, modernised; nave, of seven bays; pointed arches, octagonal piers, circular bases, octagonal caps. The font, a hexagonal cylinder. West door, of five arches, rather elaborate Flamboyant. But they are getting the anchor up. Now, men, pull;—I know it is hot; but you shall be paid well! We leap on board as the paddles begin to turn.

Selve.

And now then, what glorious beauty in this archipelago, rising from the deep purple sea! That white rounded rock, apparently quite bare of vegetation, is Pusgnac: this peaked crag, nearest of all to us, is Tovaria; the larger island, where you can just make out a white village between two pine groves, is Milada; to be distinguished carefully from the more famous Meleda, of which I shall have more to say by-and-by. And now to our left, the sunny Croatian mountains take a sudden sweep to the east, separating that province from Dalmatia; while the Dalmatian coast, as far as we see it yet, is flat and grey, hardly rising above the sea-line. Next, the eastern horizon is bounded by the Isola Grossa or Lunga; between it and ourselves, the island Uglian rises precipitously from the water; the strait contracts; and you see the spires of Zara, as the crown of the promontory which juts from the mainland, a mile ahead of us. But Zara requires another chapter.

Chapter VII.

ZARA: SEBENICO.

The vessels of the Austrian Lloyd's run with such extreme regularity between Trieste and Cattaro, and usually stay during such a very convenient time at the principal cities *en route*, that nothing is more agreeable than to avail oneself of their system. It will not be necessary to describe the particular course of our wanderings further than this: that we made our way from Zara by the "Littoral" to Cattaro, seeing what we could of the inner islands, and returning from Cattaro by the outer islands.

It may not be amiss to give a general idea of the voyages of these admirable ships. The passage is delightful; the sea is usually so sheltered as to be lake-like. The captains, who speak German, French, and Italian, besides Illyrian, are eager to do all in their power to accommodate a stranger, and ready to give every information on a route where every half hour brings a new island or scoglio into notice.

The routes are these :—

A. Trieste—Fiume.

Boat leaves Trieste every Tuesday and Saturday at 6 A. M. Running along the Istrian coast, and touching at Pirano, Umago, Citta Nova, Parenzo, it reaches Rovigno at 2 P.M.; Fasana at 3·45; Pola at 6 P.M. At Pola it lies till 10 P.M. Pursuing its way, it doubles the southern point a little before midnight: crosses the Gulf of Medolino, enters the Quarnero, and goes into the harbour of Cherso at 3·30 A.M. At 7, it touches at Malinski, in the north of Veglia, then stands north across the Bay of Fiume, and reaches that city at 9 P.M.; twenty-seven hours, including stoppages, from Trieste. It returns from Fiume at 5 P.M. every Wednesday and Sunday, reaching Trieste at 8 P.M. on Thursday and Monday.

B. Fiume—Zara.

Boat leaves Fiume at 3 A.M. every Saturday, calls at Zengh, on the Littoral, at 7·15; Besca Nuova, (S. E. of Veglia) 8·15; the island of Arbe at 11; then crossing the Quarnerulo reaches Lussin-grande on the east coast of Ossero at 1·15; Val Cassione at 5·15 P.M.; Zara, 7·45 P.M. It leaves Zara every Monday at 3 A.M., and reaches Fiume at 7·45 P.M. the same day.

C. Trieste-Cattaro line.

Boat leaves Trieste every Tuesday 4 P.M.,
Reaches	Lussinpiccolo	Wednesday	5 A.M.	Stops 3 hours.
,,	Selve	,,	10·30 A.M.	
,,	Zara	,,	2·30 P.M.	Stops 13 hours.
,,	Sebenico	Thursday	9 A.M.	,, 3½ ,,
,,	Spalato	,,	6 P.M.	,, 9 ,,
,,	Macarsca	Friday	7 A.M.	
,,	Curzola	,,	12 noon.	,, 1 ,,
,,	Ragusa	,,	7·30 P.M.	,, 11 ,,
,,	Megline	Saturday	10·15 A.M.	,, 1¾ ,,
,,	Perasto	,,	1 P.M.	
,,	Cattaro	,,	2 P.M.	

Returns from Cattaro, Sunday, 8 A.M.; reaches Trieste Thursday.

D. Dalmato-Albanese.

Boat leaves Trieste every Saturday noon,

Reaches Zara	Sunday 5 A.M.		Stops	5 hours.	
,, Sebenico	,,	5·30 P.M.	,,	12	,,
,, Spálato	Monday 9·30 A.M.		,,	2½	,,
,, Milna	,,	1·30 P.M.	,,	1	,,
,, Lesina	,,	4·30 P.M.	,,	1	,,
,, Curzola	,,	9·30 P.M.			
,, Gravosa	Tuesday 4 A.M.				
,, Perasto	,,	5·30 P.M.			
,, Cattaro	,,	6.45 P.M.			

Leaves Cattaro Wednesday, and reaches Corfu Friday.
Leaves Cattaro every Tuesday, 6 A.M.
Reaches Trieste ,, Saturday, 5 A.M.

The "Pyroscaphs" of the Dalmato-Albanese line as being the stronger, take the outer islands; the Trieste-Cattaro the inner.

These times were arranged in June 1857, and were kept to in the May of the present year. Singularly enough, the hours of arrival are not published: the little *Itinerario Maritimo* simply gives the days. I have printed the hours as I copied them into my own Itinerario from the official book of an Austrian Lloyd's clerk.

It was on a Wednesday, at 2 P.M. that we cast anchor off Zara. A very picturesque city is the capital of Dalmatia, seen from the water, and crowded within its Venetian walls. The low hills round it were baking in the excessive fervour of an Adriatic sun, but the distant heights of Vellebitchi looked cool and pleasant. We entered by a gate that carries the lion of S. Mark, and found ourselves in the narrow lanes, so cool, and yet so close; every door shut, scarcely an inhabitant out of doors; the whole place given up to its siesta. When will the churches be open? *Signor*, at 4. When will the booksellers' shops be open? *Signor*, at 4. Can we get any ice? *Signor*, at 4. We whiled away the two hours by exploring the exterior of the public buildings. The sea-gate, called the Porta di S. Grisogono, is Roman; but it was brought from Œnona. The inscription is—

MELIA. ANNIANA. IN. MEMOR. Q. LÆPICI. Q. F. SERG. BASSI.
MARITI. SUI
IMPORIVM. STERM. ET. ARCUM. FIERI. ET. STATUAS. SUPERIMPONI.
TEST. JVSS. EX. IIS. DCDXXI . , . .

The population of Zara is about 7,000. Two Corinthian columns exist; one at the Piazza della Erbe—this has the chains still remaining by which prisoners were bound to it. The other is by S. Simeon's.

The principal bookseller is the firm of Brattara, brothers; who have excellent founts both of Latin and Cyrillic types. Here I spent, one day, two most agreeable hours, making inquiries with respect to Illyrian literature, and purchasing ecclesiastical books. Two of the works published by them are very useful for the stranger in Zara. They are, Professor Potter's *Compendio Geografico della Dalmazia:* the other a mere brochure, *Sull' Architettura delle Chiese di Zara, del Professor Georgio Vonbank.*

I will first speak of the Cathedral, of which the accompanying plate represents the western façade. The cathedral, metropolitical, and primatial church of Zara was erected in the thirteenth century by the French and Venetian crusaders, as a propitiatory

offering for their sacrilegious* destruction of many
churches in this same city. It is a normal specimen of
Lombardo-Romanesque, and was consecrated in 1285.

It is of the simplest plan. Chancel and nave, both
with aisles. Tower north of choir.

Zara Cathedral.
The apse is semi-circular, and quite plain.
The altar stands at its west end under a
baldachin; erected in 1322. The four piers,

1	2
3	4

are all circular on square base. 1, is chevronnée, and

* The letters of Innocent III. to Dandolo and his companions,
on the occasion of the capture of Zara, may be seen in Raynaldus,
1202. iii, iv.

very much resembles those in the Galilee at Durham; 2 is worked in spiral mouldings; 3 is checkie; 4 is wrought in circular bosses, with interstitial flowers. The arches are concealed with paltry red hangings, as we shall find in most of the Dalmatian churches. The arches themselves are pointed; the vaulting is quite plain. The bishop's seat, at the east end of the synthronus, remains, with two arms. On each side of the choir are sixteen stalls, elaborate early arabesque, with subsellæ. At the top of the canopy work over each is a little semi-figure holding a scroll with the name of the stall. The pavement of the choir is rather inferior mosaic. It is raised on a crypt, with the usual arrangement; a central ascending staircase; two side descending flights of steps. Of this I will speak presently.

The choir-aisles have three bays. The piers of the central arch are circular, with square base, and Corinthianizing capitals. Those to the east and west are six-clustered.

The nave has seven bays; the caps square and Corinthianizing.

The piers themselves—

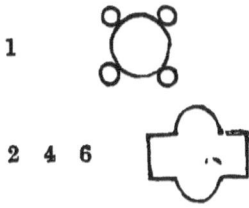

1

2 4 6

3 Circular.
5 Circular, voluted.

All these have the most wretched red hangings.

The roof is now flat ceiled. The apse arch and chancel arch very plain. The aisle windows are blocked. There are three very small clerestory lights over each arch; over these is a series of vile modern stable windows, large semi-circles.

In the north chancel aisle, nearly blocked off from the choir, I thought the following modern tablets worth copying:

> Alex. III. Pont. Opt. Max.
> Anno 1177
> Super equum album
> Jaderam ingredienti
> Canticis Illyricis a clero salutato
> Sepulcrum S. Anastasiæ invisenti
> et colenti.

> Valerio Episcop. Jadr..
> qui cum aliis patribus Palladium damnavit et Jovinianum :
> Lampridio de Gallelis Jadr.
> qui anno 1146 metropolitano titulo ac jure suam ditavit ecclesiam :.
> Petro de Malapharis Jadr.
> qui, ad Dei cultum augendum, anno D. 1395, capitulum restituit :
> Maphæo Vallareso Venet
> qui sæculo XV turrim struxit, templum restauravit
> ornavitque :
> atque piissimo Bernardo Claio Veneto
> et doctissimo Vincentio Zmaievitch Antibarensi,.
> quorum alter sæculo xvii. ad Latinos,.
> alter sequenti seculo ad Illyricos clericos
> Seminaria fundaverunt
> Fabricæ a consilio   III viri
> P.P.

Of these seminaries we shall presently hear something more. There is another tablet to S. Anastasia, the patron of the church.

The crypt is very singular. Answering in its

circular east end to the superincumbent edifice, it has three small oblong slits for windows. Four piers curve round the eastern end of the apse; they have circular shafts on square base, and heavy square caps. In one of these piers is a grated aperture, as if for relics. The original altar remains now utterly desecrated. In the front is a female figure, with long hair over the breast, and holding two trees, or poles; the legend, so far as a wretched taper allowed me to see, Santa Aššā. The crypt itself has seven bays; the second being distinguished by the pointed tympana of the arches. Of all this, Potter and Vonbank say nothing; and Sir G. Wilkinson scarcely mentions the crypt. The sacristan told me that the Emperor was about to have it restored. I hope that the restoration may be worthy of the place; a most remarkable and valuable example of such a crypt. Having made these notes, I gladly rejoined my companion in the nave; and we attended the first vespers of the coming festival (Holy Thursday). There was a fair attendance of Canons, a few scholars from the seminaries, and a good number of poor women. The choir was in a wretched west gallery; the service was well and reverently sung.

The following were my notes of the north side, externally; the south side is only accessible from the seminary. It has seven bays, divided by Romanesque-like flat buttresses; in each, an elegant, very acutely pointed trefoil. Above these is an arcade-passage of five arches to each bay; arches circular, shafts octagonal with square cap. The clerestory is a succession of circular-headed arches, corbelled off, nebule-wise; a very good and rich effect.

The tower, built in 1496, is very massy, and rather clumsy, of three stages. The uppermost, a very low pyramidal head, with square apertures. The next, two large open belfry windows, the shaft circular, with square base and cap. The western façade will be best described in the plate. The south side differs in no remarkable way from the north, except in having one elegant rose.

We were extremely anxious to see Archbishop Godeassi; but he was in the country. We therefore called at the Zmaievitch Seminary. This is the educational institution founded by that excellent prelate,—he sat from 1713-1746,—for Illyrian-speaking Priests. And thanks to our letter of recommendation, we received a warm welcome from the Very Reverend Rector Demetrius Stipcevich. Of him, I made many inquiries with respect to the Glagolita rite; with the result of which the reader has already been made acquainted. In the eight classes of this institution are thirty-three students: judging from their behaviour to ourselves, we are bound to speak highly of their courtesy and affability. One of them, by name John Mottussich, was so good as to accompany us in most of our other researches.

Zara S. Maria. Hence we went to the Benedictine Convent of *S. Maria*. The church stands back in a small court; it is almost entirely modernised, but in the western façade is a small rose of sixteen trefoiled lights. The tower is, what would seem a usual position here, to the north of the church; and consists of four stages. The belfry stage has, under a low pyramidal head, four adjacent circular-headed lights, set in a sunk panel. The second and third have each two sets of two circular-headed lights, divided by buttresses. The lowest stage is perfectly plain, but very high. This tower, though it possesses little beauty, is yet valuable, because the exact date is known. It was finished by Coloman, King of Hungary, in 1105, after he had conquered Dalmatia. The nunnery was founded, in 1066, by a sister of King Cresimir, of Croatia.

Next to *S. Grisogono.* This, next to the Cathedral, is the most interesting place in the city. They give it a date anterior to the ninth century; and undoubtedly it is of very great antiquity. It consists simply of chancel, nave, and aisles, with tower at the north-west of the nave; the whole arrangement much resembles that of the Cathedral. It is triapsidal. The central apse is perfectly plain and circular; the choir, which consists of two bays, is approached by five steps; the nave has five bays. The shafts are circular with square Corinthianizing capitals; the bases square, with heads at the corners. The vaulting shafts have been cut away; as, I should have remarked, they were at the Cathedral. The aisle-apses are blocked from the interior; the apse arches, however, remain, circular of two very simple square orders. The synthronus is modern; the roof, flat; and there is no clerestory. The string above the arches, which are not in the least modernised, consists of an edge-wise chevron. The south side is very remarkable; it is divided in twelve arches with voluted shafts. Standing at the east end, we find the triapsidal arrangement perfect: the side apses had one plain,

Zara S. Grisogono.

circular-headed light; the central apse is pannelled in five divisions by four slender shafts, all of them circular, with square base and square cap; some voluted. Above this is an elegant arcade like that of the side of the Cathedral, which seems to have been a real triforium; there are seventeen arches; five of them contain small circular-headed slits; the work is very pretty; the eastern gable of the arches is nebuly. The western façade has also its gable nebuly; then an arcade of nine circular-headed lights; the central one twice as thick as the others, and alone pierced. The door has a circular head, with four orders, and a projecting gable above. The tower is so much like that of the cathedral that a separate description is unnecessary. It was erected, as I said, in 1105; but must have been much modernised.

Hence we went to the Greek church, S. Elias, originally a Latin building, and only given up to the Greeks during the French invasion. Previously they had occupied one of its chapels alone. Here we dispatched Dundich to inquire if we could pay our respects to the Greek Bishop; and after a great many preliminary inquiries as to our object in so doing, we were ushered up three long flights of stone steps to his reception-room. Steven Knezevitch has been Bishop since 1853; he is a remarkably interesting person, tall and commanding. He wore a rich black cassock, scarlet stockings, girdle, and skull cap, and a gold pectoral cross. The seminary, in which he takes great interest, has five good professors, and about forty students. The head, or economus, as he is called, of the clerical "convict," where the young men board together, and are bound by certain regulations, is Sebastian Lukovitch. With such a diocese as Dalmatia, with its northern and southern extremities so far apart, and its priests scattered at such distances from each other, the Bishop has found it necessary to establish a pro-vicar at Cattaro, who is Archimandrite at the Praskevitch monastery; and whom I afterwards had the pleasure of seeing. By what we could learn, the Greek priests have very much improved in attainments during the last twenty years; and it is now a rare thing to find one who is only acquainted with Illyrian. The Protopopes especially are generally speaking of high attainments; there are eight: respectively situated at Zara, with 12,340 orthodox; at Scardona, with 12,092; at Knin, with 18,620; at Sebenico, with 5,742; at Imoschi, with 7,790; at Castelnovo, with 12,347; at Cattaro, with 7,838; at Budua, with 5,360. I see that, in the course of the preceding year, five deacons were raised to the priesthood, one clerk in inferior orders to the Diaconate, and one similar clerk both to the Diaconate and to the priesthood; also that there were four deaths among the priests, and two among the deacons. The total number of souls who acknowledge the Bishop of Zara as their prelate, is 82,717; an increase of 2,000 in the two preceding years. I was particularly requested to observe the exceedingly high morality of the people as shown by the authenticated lists of legitimate, and illegitimate births; and certainly it speaks very favourably for the state of the Greek Church in Dalmatia. Thus, in a sea-port town like Sebenico, always, of course, the least favourable example; against 242 legitimate, there are but 3 illegitimate births; at Cattaro, against 221 of the former, only 1 of the latter; at Budua, 137 of the former, and none of the latter. Even in the worst arch-presbytery, that of Zara, against 617 of the former there are only 20 of the latter. It must be remembered, however, that the Church which is in the minority will always be purer than that which is the Establishment: it is very striking to see cottages scattered here and there, tenanted by orthodox Greeks, who live among a Latin population, and who will pass the Latin church on the way to their own, to go for their sacraments six, or seven, or eight miles away. I asked the Bishop if the extreme severity of the Greek fasts, when brought into contrast with the prodigious laxity of the Latin, did not diminish the number of his people; he told me that he had no reason to attribute any such effect to that difference between the two churches. At the same time, in the wilder parts of the country, and especially among the Morlacchi, it is not easy to get an answer as to which communion they belong. The easiest method, after you have asked,—"Are you a Christian?" is to proceed—"Show me which way you make the sign of the cross."

Of the church of *S. Simeon* I have not much to say.

<small>Zara S. Simeon.</small> It is the largest next to the Cathedral, and stands boldly and well; but it is so much modernised as to have lost its interest. The shrine of the Saint beneath the High Altar, presented by Elizabeth of Hungary, and completed in 1380, at an expense of 42,000 florins, is a fine work of art, but so fenced and guarded that it is impossible to

give an ecclesiological description. S. Simeon is *Compatron* of the city.

A very interesting expedition is to be made from Zara to the Isle of Uglian, which lies opposite: in a four-oared boat it takes about an hour. This island, about twelve miles in length, by two-and-a-half in breadth, has some very pretty scenery; the dark pines which surmount its crags give a peculiarly Dalmatian character to the landscape. Landing at Oltre, a miserable little village, with a modern church, you immediately begin the ascent of S. Michael's Hill, the saint here, as everywhere else, of high places: an ascent which puts one in mind of the former part of that which leads to the summit of Cader Idris from Barmouth. The hill itself cannot be more than 800 or 1,000 feet high. But from the summit there is such a view as I suppose very few localities of Europe could afford. I can never remember the time, since I was a child, that I had not a fancy for exploring those long queer shaped Illyrian islands; but most assuredly the reality surpassed any expectation my fancy might have formed. Standing at the foot of a mass of shapeless ruins called Fort S. Michael, (among which, by-the-by, you may make out the triapsidal end of a very early church,) and facing north, you see right across the little strait, Zara, crowded together on its promontory, a forest of masts rising from its harbours; immediately beyond it the Boccagnazza and the Malpaga lines of hills, with the great Vellebitchi mountains shutting in the horizon, here and there a dazzlingly white patch of snow on their highest crests. Turning to the right, your eye traces the "canal" of Zara, between the main land and Uglian, and its neighbour island Pasman. But it is when you turn to the west that the view is most remarkable. Like a black spot in the sea rises Eso; the spire of Eso-Ponentale crowning its northern mainland. The horizon is shut in by the long hill lines of Isola Grossa; saw-like serrated edges, with dark blotches of firs. But to the left of Eso, and between yourself and Isola Grossa, are a quantity of little islands or Scoglii; sometimes rising like mere sandbanks above the blue waters, sometimes in sharp points, sometimes in conical projections. Thus, you see, further to the left hand, Sit; then Lopes; then, with one or two houses on it, Labdara, then Vacca Velica: while to the right, there are Zvirinas, and Sestrugn, and Rivagn.

It was a very pretty sight, too, as we walked up and down the deck, late at night, a fine warm May night, to see the twinkling lights that marked out the boundaries of the city, and to watch the phosphoric blaze that sprang from every stroke, and the beads of blue light that dripped from every oar, as the boats darted across the harbour. The cathedral rang its Angelus at ten o'clock; but after that time we could make out the lighted windows, which showed that some service was going on in Santa Maria.

I have put down here, as I shall continue to do hereafter, what happened to us in two separate visits to Zara, as if the whole had occurred at one time. It was very early on Ascension Day, about half-past five in the morning, that I made my way on deck at our first visit to our next point of interest, Sebenico. We were then running through a very narrow strait, with the Weichsel wood covering the mainland to the left, and the two little islands of Tilvat and Parvich to our right. On Parvich, there is a village called Luca, the church of which, as I made it out with a telescope of great power, seems interesting. Every moment the scenery increased in beauty; the woods cleared away, and a pretty cultivated country took their place; we next passed the island of Slarin, and our vessel, then turning north, went in through a strait not a quarter of a mile broad, to the inland gulf of Sebenico; on the opposite side of which rose the city—a city more striking in its first appearance than even Zara.

The extreme beauty of the Dalmatian dress had struck us both; and I was informed that Sebenico was the most likely place to procure a complete example of it. As there are no shops in which such dresses are to be obtained ready made, Dundich made one or two attempts by addressing himself to women who were keeping stalls in the streets, to discover how I should be able to get what I wanted. It happened that just as an old lady was resenting his inquiries as an insult, a canon of the cathedral, an elderly man, passed by. By good fortune he spoke German; and on hearing what I was in pursuit of, said that he thought that from one woman or another of his parish —for he had a large parish,—he could obtain for us the dress in question. Accordingly he led us into a spacious back yard, surrounded on all sides by tall houses; and addressing a woman who was up to her elbows in soap-suds, told her what I was seeking, and promised her a florin if she could get a perfect collection then and there, of a Dalmatian peasant woman's dress. In about half an hour we were surrounded by women, bringing various articles of apparel, concerning which I only insisted that they all should be new. A chair was brought out into the yard for the purpose of being vested; and our good friend the canon, heartily amused, made the selection of apparel, and drove our bargain. Meanwhile, every window in the houses which overlooked the yard, was crowded with spectators; and two ladies who came on parochial business after the canon, expressed their great surprise at finding him thus engaged. It is miserable to see how, in the upper classes, the beautiful Dalmatian costume has given way to crinoline, and all the second-rate finery of Paris or London. The articles which I bought, and their price, were as follows: they form the complete dress of a Dalmatian woman.

1. The Kušulja, or shift, with square surplice-like sleeves, embroidered with red and green silk round the neck, and at the back of the arm, with a narrow line of red silk in front of the arm—4 florins. The material, the very coarsest linen.

2. The Bernijça. This is a dress of red or green moreen, of the coarsest kind, open in front, bound round the neck and arms with counter-changed green or red cloth; and edged round the bottom in a similar manner. Thus the sleeves and front of the Kušulja are shown in contrast with it: 10 florins.

3. Kaniça. A girdle of thick, many-coloured braid, tied in a knot at the left side: 1 florin, 34 cents.

4. Bicque, or stockings of red worsted: 4 florins.

5. Kappa. A cap of red cloth, embroidered all round with black silk, with a short fringe on the forehead: 2 florins.

6 and 7. Oguza and Maitte; neck riband and clasp, the clasp of silver gilt (but very often, even amongst the poorest peasants of gold, and sometimes jewelled) the riband of white linen, embroidered with gold, red and blue: 5 florins (but they are often worth 50).

8. Kefizza, or purse, a small, flat, stiff bag of red and white worsted mixed with gold. This is tucked in between the Kusulja, and the Bernijça, so that the fringe just appears at the left side of the neck, 6c.

9. Pregliazza, or apron, of worsted, as thick as carpet, striped horizontally in different colours, and fringed half way down the sides and at the bottom: 4 florins.

10. Shoes of yellow, green, or red leather. The front of the Kusulja is, in the case of married women covered with a piece of red cloth; but girls wear, attached to it, their future dowry in florins; so that, in making your proposal to a Dalmatian peasant girl, you can tell at once how much money she will bring you.

Having settled this important matter, we were at liberty to turn our attention to the churches of Sebenico, which I now proceed to describe:

The *Cathedral of Sebenico*, of which the accompanying is an external view, is, in its way, the most remarkable building I ever saw. It is a mixture of Flamboyant and Re- *Sebenico Cathedral.*

naissance, which would seem to promise nothing but

imbecility of *motif*, and overgorgeousness of decoration. Whereas, in truth it is one of the noblest, most striking, most simple, most Christian of churches, and, though highly ornamented, such is the sublimity of its design, that it gives you the impression of being by no means richly decorated. Both times that I saw it, I saw it under a great disadvantage; it was undergoing a thorough (and very good) restoration, and the interior was filled with scaffolding. Of course, cathedrals, such as Pola, Parenzo, and Spalato, have a much deeper and more enthusiastic interest than anything which mere architecture can give. But in an exclusively architectural view, I do not hesitate to call this the most interesting church in Dalmatia. And the more so on this account: that the whole idea and the details must stand or fall together. You could not translate it into Middle-Pointed. I have frequently made a mental attempt at doing so, and have every time felt that the task was impossible.

The cathedral stands at the north end of the city, and forms a somewhat conspicuous object from the sea. It is dedicated to S. James. The first stone was laid by Bishop Giorgio Sisgorio, a native of Sebenico; and after being carried on by Urbano Vignaco, Luca Tolentic, Francesco Quirino, Bartolomeo Bonnio, and Giovanni Stafileo, but without any very great progress having been made, was continued in real earnest by Giovanni Il-Lucie Stafileo, a native of Trau, who succeeded to the episcopate in 1528, consecrated the finished building on April 28, 1555, and died in 1557. In 1564 the first diocesan synod of Sebenico was convoked in it by Bishop Girolamo Saviniano, who was one of the Fathers of Trent. The synod must have been a small one, for, as we shall see, from the present diocese of Sebenico, the then Bishoprics of Knin and Scardona must be subtracted.

Let me describe it as well as I can. The apse, which is circular, has five sets of double trefoiled windows, with very elaborate tracery. The sacristy consists of one bay, ascended by seven steps, and fenced in by a low stone screen, the shafts, volute-wise, with Corinthianizing caps. Now comes the choir, under a very lofty dome, and flanked on each side by a wide open space, rather than aisles. The stalls, which are of stone, are not divided. A very singular effect is given by the passages which run behind and above the stalls to the ambones; the latter, as well as the passages themselves, have rails like those that inclose the sanctuary. The choir is ascended by six steps. The nave has six bays: the piers circular, caps square and quasi-Romanesque, pointed arches. The triforium is a square-headed semi-classical arcade, the clerestory also renaissance; under the former a very rich flower moulding. The vaulting is lofty, of plain barrel: exceedingly bold. Some of the stones which compose it are twelve feet by three feet six. The west end has an elaborate rose of 24 leaves; above that, a smaller one of twelve. The aisle-vaulting is simply cross: some of the ribs voluted. The west door is exceedingly rich, but a very curious mixture of cinquecento and Flamboyant. The crypt at the south of the choir is the baptistery. It is a circle, so to speak, inserted in a square; each side of the square formed by a very rich arch: circular shafts, flowered caps. A classical shell conceals each of the four junctions. Above each of these is some of the noblest Flamboyant work I ever saw. The font, merely classical, and supported by boys. The strangeness of this work culminates undoubtedly in the baptistery.

S. Maria di Valle Verde. Hence we went to *Valle Verde*,—a church on the outskirts of the city. It has a flat panelled roof: in the centre, the *Incoronazione*. The arrangement not bad. In a western gallery of marble is this inscription:—

> Regum Rege J. C. Ao. 1629. d. 23 Apr. Vincentius Arrigonius Sibenecensis Episcop. Templum hoc et altare

majus ad honorem Dei et Beatæ Mariæ Virginis
includens in eodem Altari reliquias S. Joannis Bapt.
S. Thomæ Apostoli, et S. Barbaræ, Virgin. et Martyris,
consecravit: curante Paulo Cassio
superiore.

The *Madonna di Borgo* was perhaps an early church. Square chancel, nave, north chapel; south tower detached, but connected with the church by an arch. At the west end, a rose of eight leaves; above it, a smaller one. A south door is dated 1509. The tower has four stages, with a pyramidal spire. Madonna di Borgo.

We then went to the *Dominican Convent*, founded in 1346, but entirely modernised. Here we saw the Ascension Procession start; there seemed a great deal of devotion among the people. On a second visit, the Prior, Paolo Bioni, ex-Provincial of the Order, was exceedingly kind to me. While I was engaged in copying sequences, he ordered wine and biscuits to be served; and here, as always, the good Fathers proved themselves excellent vine-cultivators. The church is on the *motif* of the Cathedral.

The *Franciscan Convent* I only saw by night. It is said to have been founded, in 1320, by Adam, one of the original companions of the great Patriarch of the Order. Some of the original work remains, especially the cloisters on the south, very elegant. It was impossible to take a detailed account of this church, because the exposition of some celebrated relic was going on, and the whole was crowded with worshippers, anxious on their knees to kiss it.

We also saw *S. Pasquale*, outside the city to the west: and the Benedictine Nunnery of S. Lucia, finished in 1639. The school was shown me by one of the Sisters, Maria Angela Brazzetti; it seemed in admirable order.

We left Sebenico at noon, on a bright day. After winding our way through the narrow canal of S. Antonio, we passed S. Nicolo to our left; the island of Zlavni, or Slavi, with its fir groves, lying close to our right. It contains about 1840 inhabitants; the church, under the Invocation of Santa Maria Assunta, is modern. Threading then our way between the tiny islands of Gherbuia and Deruvenika, both uninhabited, and catching to the left, the little village tower of Crapano island, we stood south-west, Mount Tartari here pushing out his giant rocks far into the sea. A dark, grim, pine-covered mountain he looked; and the coast is here iron-bound. Past the island of S. Simeon; then between Smoquizza and the main; then Mastignac to our right, and the grey old village of Cas Cesto to our left; past the islands Simoskoi and Muja; doubled Cape S. Zuane, with the monastery towering out from one of the spurs of Tartari. After this, we leave the mainland for a while, and pass between the large island of Bua, of which I shall have more to say, to the left; and Solta to the right. As we coast the latter, it looks lovely in the declining sun; and one bay especially, Val de Mezzo, dwells on my memory, even now, as a rare vision of beauty. Presently, beyond Point Pusniz in Bua, the littoral opens again, and far, far off, I catch the high tower of the once Temple of Jupiter, now the Cathedral Church of Spalăto.

Chapter VIII.

SPALATO.

Yes, Spalăto not Spalāto; and still less, as we so commonly find it written, Spalatro. The name is simply derived from the palace of Diocletian.

And what were our thoughts, as we ran up the canal of Sobas, and every moment that great tower rose higher and higher? What but of poor Mark Antony de Dominis?

Let me tell you, gentle reader, his sad history.

Late in August, 1602, there came news to Rome that the see of Spalato was vacant. The Dominicans said a few masses for their brother Dominic Marescotti, of good memory, late Archbishop; the Cardinals inquired what the place was worth; the Venetian ambassador was on the look out for instructions; the canons of S. Jerome of the Illyrians in the City said that it was a shame to appoint any man not acquainted with the language. Several candidates were in the field: for to be Metropolitan and Primate of all Dalmatia was something, though the see, tossed about as it had been from Constantinople to Hungary, from Naples to Bosnia, from the Ban of Croatia to the Doge of Venice, was worth comparatively little. In a few days, Cardinal Cinthio was waited on by the Bishop of Zengh;* his name, Mark Antony de Dominis. He had the votes of the Chapter in his favour; an Illyrian by birth, he could speak the language fluently; the Serene Republic was not averse; he would endeavour to do his duty if promoted, and he hoped for his Illustrious Reverence's† protection. He was introduced to the Pope; and the Consistorial Acts tell us that, on the 15th of November, M. Antony was absolved from his bond to the Church of Zengh, and translated to Spalato.

Before this, however, it began to be whispered that the Archbishop had some singular views. He was bent on residence and hard work. He had certain uncomfortable notions on the immediate derivation of episcopal authority from CHRIST, and he absolutely declared his intention of preaching every day of the ensuing Lent to his people. The thing was really *outré;* nobody ever did so now; he might preach, after celebrating pontifically, now and then, if he liked, but a daily sermon was impossible. "Why so?" inquired De Dominis. "Chrysostom and Gregory could do it, why not I?" "But no one knows in what vestments you ought to preach," they persisted. "Then I will find out," was the rejoinder. And accordingly, "The Sacred Congregation of Rites replied, that he must preach in his ordinary and every day habit, in

* Zengh, in Austrian Croatia is the place of which I have spoken above. The reader must not confound the Episcopus *Seniensis* with the Ep. Senensis (Sienna) or Signinus (Segni in the Campagna.) De Dominis's doings at Zengh are supplied by Farlati, Illyr. Sacr. iv. 137.

† The title of Eminence was first given by Urban VIII.

rochet and *mozzetta*, with stole, unless he has celebrated High Mass previously, in which case the form of the ceremonial is to be observed; and thus it declared Nov. 13, 1602."

De Dominis did not, however, get his see without having a pension assigned thereon of five hundred ducats to his competitor Andreucci, who soon after was made Bishop of Traugurium, and so one of the suffragans of Spalato. News presently came to Rome of a furious quarrel between these two. The Archbishop refused to pay the pension for a year of pestilence, the Bishop insisted on all. De Dominis found himself suspended from his functions by the Auditor of the Apostolic Chamber, and this occurred on two different occasions from the same cause. Sequestration from the pastoral office gave more time for study, and no doubt the foundations of the *De Republicâ Ecclesiasticâ* were laid in that retirement. "Here am I," reasoned De Dominis, "a primate, in a country where Pastoral superintendence is, if anywhere, essential, suspended on account of a debt which was at first made so in violation of the canons,—and is now enforced in spite of the facts. And yet we talk of the equality of Bishops, and claim to hold discipline unchanged from primitive times!" And who shall say that he did not reason aright? Granted that De Dominis was somewhat of an archæologist, had he not provocation enough in a piece of oppression which endangered the souls of his flock, to confirm him in his primitivism? And when shortly afterwards, he issued twenty-two constitutions for his diocese, and the Sacred Congregation either absolutely, or partially, annulled eighteen, must he not have contrasted his own situation with that of the earlier bishops, whose names were as his household words?

Soon after Andreucci and his Metropolitan had another contest, which (whoever were right on the point disputed, the condemnation of some clerks by the former, and their absolution by the latter), brings out the early system of true metropolitical powers as strongly held by the Primate, and brings out, also, a great deal of unseemly violence on the part of both. "Saul, Saul,"*—thus the Archbishop commences—

> "Why persecutest thou me? It is hard for thee to kick against the pricks. Have you not yet lost your military spirit,—though by a leap you passed from the sword to the pastoral staff? Away, my brother, away with earthly conversation,—and now at length casting aside the warfare of this world, enroll yourself after a far different sort in the armies of CHRIST. Put on the manners, the arms, the spirit that become a soldier, nay, rather, a general and præfect of CHRIST. If it seem intolerable to you that you are in subjection to me, seek another see; and that not *any* other, but the Supreme and Apostolic, if you would pay obedience to none. Confound not, my brother, I pray you, the order of Ecclesiastical Hierarchy."

All through one sees the character of the man: resolute, and indeed, overbearing in defence of a principle; naturally falling back on early examples, and living more in primitive times than his own; disposed to make no allowance for the altered condition of his own church, and abhorring development. Having occasion to rebuild the choir of his cathedral, he reintroduced the *synthronus;* and being blamed for raising

---

* Farlati, Illyric. Sacr. tom. iii. p. 489.

himself higher than the altar, he met the objection by erecting over the latter a most ponderous *ciborium*.

He soon gave another proof of his wish to return to primitive use. The clergy of Spalato were in a very corrupt state; and a fresh element of difficulty was to be found in the use of the two languages, Latin and Illyrico-Slavonic. A priest only acquainted with the former was perhaps sent into a parish where the latter was employed; or *vice versâ*. Now, it needed not De Dominis's reading to be aware that, in early times, no one was admitted into the lists of the clergy without having the voice of the people in favour of his general good character and fitness for the office. But even the Archbishop dared not venture on this; he, therefore, cast about for an expedient that might reconcile primitive strictness and modern laxity. At last he hit on the plan that all candidates for Holy Orders should undergo an examination before the Chapter,— and that on its result a ballot should be taken. This seemed to produce good effects; but, in two years, the Archbishop proceeded much further. He now ordered that all the priests (I suppose of the city, not of the diocese) should be 'discussed' by the Chapter on occasion of every ordination, and that such as were thought unworthy of their office should be suspended. This, it need not be said, is as much opposed to primitive as to ultramontane custom. Hence curious records in the Chapter Acts. For example:—

" And so the Clerk, Gregory de Benedictis, was first discussed; and he had all the votes, namely fourteen, in his favour, and none against him. Francis Orsillo had, in like manner, all the votes in his favour, and none against him. Innocent Chahich had thirteen votes against him, and one in his favour. The said Innocent was excluded from the Clergy. Francis Manoli had twelve votes in his favour, and two against him, &c."

It is only wonderful that the excluded clergy did not appeal to Rome.

In the meantime, De Dominis was wearied out with the usurpations and encroachments of the apostolic see, and meditated the bold step of leaving his post, and throwing off her jurisdiction. That he did not act hastily, though he might have acted injudiciously, cannot be denied. His three enormous folios *de Republicâ Ecclesiasticâ* were published in 1617: and could hardly have been commenced later than 1607. In the meantime, his sermons, to which multitudes thronged, contained expressions, bolder and bolder, against Roman supremacy, till at length a hearer exclaimed, at the conclusion of one of his assertions on that subject, "You lie in your throat." It was more than whispered that the Archbishop was a heretic; and that steps ought to be taken to procure his deposition. Let us see what was his own state of mind:—

"From the Episcopate I was raised to the Archiepiscopate. Hence, a new and more urgent occasion of renewing my studies (of the Fathers as contradistinguished from later writers), and of labouring with greater zeal and energy in them. For when the troubles occasioned me by my suffragans, and, much more, the excessive power of the Roman Court, threw every metropolitical right into confusion, I found it necessary to investigate the root and origin of all ecclesiastical degrees, powers, offices, and dignities —and especially of the Papacy. Then came the interdict of Venice. The books, written on behalf of Rome, treated us, Bishops of the Venetian dominions, as rude and unlearned beasts.

Hence, to finish my defence, and to come to the truth of the Venetian matter, a fresh occasion of new and more vigorous study. The sacred and ancient Canons, the orthodox Councils, the discipline of the Fathers, the former customs of the Church, all passed in review before me. I found in these, and these only, that for which I was looking, and far more than I had expected to find. . . . . It was once an article of faith that the Universal Church, scattered throughout the world, is that Catholic Church of CHRIST, to which CHRIST himself has promised His perpetual presence, and which Paul calls the pillar and ground of the truth. Our present Romans have contracted this article, so that by the Catholic Church they understand the Roman Court, and in that, or rather in the Pope alone, the whole spirit of CHRIST resides. And whatever has at any time been said in honour of the Catholic Church, they, with the utmost force and injury, circumscribe to the Court of Rome."*

A man who could thus think, and who was accustomed to speak out, must have found Spalato no safe place. Accordingly towards the conclusion of 1615, he suddenly went to Venice, probably undetermined what future course to pursue. In what immediately followed, some secret springs of action must have been involved, which it is now impossible to detect. Rome could not have been ignorant of De Dominis's sentiments. Yet we find him resigning his see to his kinsman, Sforza Ponzoni, and Paul V confirming the deed: and still the ex-prelate retained the title of Archbishop of Spalato in all his works. A touching epistle of his to the Spalatese is still extant, in which he maintains his attachment to the Catholic faith,— upbraids them with their cruel misapprehension of his teaching, and earnestly prays them to elect for their new Archbishop some one who should be acquainted with the Illyrian language.

* De Republicâ Christ. tom. i. § 8 of the unpaged Introduction.

At Venice, De Dominis became acquainted with the English ambassador; and hence Roman writers take occasion to reproach him with having sold his faith and soul for a pension; just as English writers accuse him of returning to Rome because his promotion was less than he had expected. Bitter words and cruel insinuations are, however, no proofs. Granted that Spalato was not an opulent see,—still its wealth was greater than anything which De Dominis could reasonably expect in a foreign country. Besides, with his learning and talents, to which such ample justice is done by his adversaries, to what might he not aspire? To any Venetian see,—to the "Patriarchate" of Venice,—to a Cardinalate,—why not to the Papacy itself? And in England, too, with his known sentiments on the necessity of a prelate speaking the language of his flock,—how could he even wish for a bishopric? No;—doubtless the ambassador, aware that such a secession would bring great credit to his church, sounded the Archbishop's mind, and framed his suggestions accordingly. De Dominis spoke of the primitive model. "The very thing," cries his Excellency, "to which we have reformed ourselves. Look—here, in the canons,—and here, in the rubrics,—and here, in the ordinal,—we refer to it expressly." The Archbishop spoke of the innovations of Rome. "We reject them all," cries the Ambassador. "No denial of the chalice — no shameless sale of indulgences—no reserves—no annates—no bishops by the grace of the apostolic see— no pallium—no interdicts." De Dominis spoke of sees *in commendam*, bishops that had ten cathedrals, and had never seen one; cardinals that heaped up canonries, and deaneries, and abbacies of distant lands. "All those corruptions gone too," says his Excellency. Then as to the election of bishops,—how was that? "By the Dean and Chapter," replies the Ambassador, "after invocation of the HOLY GHOST;" —the recommendation and præmunire being conveniently dropped. And so, little by little, the mind of De Dominis seems to have been filled with visions of a Primitive National Church, holding the catholic faith in its fullness, and yet rejecting all the novelties of the Roman Court. Two things more may be observed. The first, that a vernacular service would occasion no difficulty to the Archbishop, himself accustomed to the Illyric Missal and Breviary. The second, that in close contact with the eastern church, a married clergy would not shock his prejudices. He resolved, then, to fly to England. But this was not so easily done.

On the 23rd of August, 1616, he received the agreement of the Pope to the election of Ponzoni, together with a pension of 700 ducats. The reason of this unusual favour to a suspected man must remain a mystery. At the beginning of September, he left Venice, giving out that it was his intention to visit the principal cities of Italy. By slow journeys he bent his course to the Grisons; and from Coire, in the middle of October, he addressed a short letter to the Doge, in which he stated his sentiments on the usurpations of Rome, explained that he could neither live safely nor rule freely when within the influence of that Court, professed his unaltered affection to the

Republic, and said,—" This my necessary secession is so far from involving a secession from the holy, pure, uncorrupted, Catholic and Apostolic Faith, that in its behalf I am ready to pour forth, not ink only, but my blood, and my life itself, if need shall require."

From Coire he proceeded to Heidelberg, (where he published his *suæ profectionis consilium*,*) and thence to London. His arrival made a great sensation. He was presented at court, received as a guest by Abbot, visited Oxford and Cambridge, and was invited to assist at an episcopal consecration.† His first publication in England was his *Scoglia del naufragio Cristiano*, but the *De Republicâ* must have been put to press at once, because it appeared in the same year. This enormous work, containing upwards of 2,000 pages, obtained an immediate European reputation.‡ Intricate and perplexed as is the style, unwieldy as is the learning, tedious as is the aggregation of references, it is nevertheless a κτῆμα ἐς ἀεί. It is a kind of quarry whence almost everything that can be urged against Ultramontanism may be extracted. That a work which would make twenty-four fair octavo volumes should be republished, is not to be expected; but still no English divine is ac-

---

* This is printed at the beginning of the *De Republicâ*. There is an English translation, under the title of *A Manifestation of the Motives, &c.* published in London, by John Bill, 1616. It is very spirited, but so excessively free as to lead to the idea that a corrected copy of the Latin must have been used.

† The consecration of Nicolas Felton for Bristol, and George Montaigne for Lincoln, Dec. 14, 1617.

‡ The sentiments which Cyril Lucar entertained of it, may be seen in the letters he addressed to De Dominis, as given in my " History of Alexandria," vol. ii. p. 390.

quainted with all that can be said for his own Church, who has not studied this book. We have an *à fortiori* of 230 years since its publication, but that does not diminish its value. It obtained for its author the Mastership of the Savoy, and the Deanery of Windsor.

There is no great difficulty in tracing the workings of De Dominis's mind, which terminated in his leaving England. This national church that had reformed itself on the primitive model, in the year after his arrival sent delegates—one of them too a bishop—to the synod of Dort. The acts of that assembly were not precisely those of S. Cyprian or of S. Basil. Abbot, perhaps the worst archbishop that ever filled the chair of Canterbury, carried matters with a high hand. A majority of the leading theologians were Calvinists, spoke of the successor of S. Peter as Antichrist, and gloried in their isolation from the rest of Christendom. What De Dominis sought,—*Jerusalem, quæ ædificatur ut civitas cujus participatio ejus in idipsum,*—was not to be found on earth. He looked back to the Roman obedience—the nurse of his early years. The Spanish ambassador too played a double part. To the archbishop he enlarged on the heresy of England; to King James he discoursed on the Popery of the exile. Nor were there wanting assurances that Gregory XV was not in the same sentiments with his predecessor. The fault of a temporary secession would be more than expiated by the glory of a lasting return. " Perhaps he therefore departed for a season, that thou shouldest receive him for ever ; not now as a servant, but above

L

a servant; a brother beloved." The old man—he was now sixty-four—yielded, and applied for leave to return to Italy. We can imagine King James saying, or swearing, that he "had na sae whaapled wi' the Paip in his younger days, whilk was weel kent o' a' Christendom, as to let the auld fule gang his ways noo." However, he appointed a commission—its prelates were Abbot of Canterbury, Neyle of Durham, Montaigne of London, Andrewes of Winchester, and Williams of Lincoln, Lord Keeper—to return what answer they thought fit. They met at Lambeth, and after hearing the archbishop's defence, commanded him to leave the kingdom in twenty days, on pain of coming under the penalties affixed by law to communications with Rome. *It is said*—and the poor archbishop has now no tongue to deny it—that he earnestly protested his entire approval of the Church of England, and promised never to speak against her. That such a promise was either given or accepted seems doubtful. The price of reconciliation with Rome must be renunciation of Canterbury, and the Roman formula for such a process was not likely to be a very gentle one. Would that we could know what Andrewes thought of all this! Abbot was an ultra-Calvinist; Neyle, a courtier; Montaigne, a bon-vivant; Williams, a man devoured with ambition; and they did as one might expect.

De Dominis went to Brussels, and there waited for a safe conduct, which never came. During his six months' residence in that city, he is said frequently to have lamented—and naturally enough—his unhappy journey to England. He at length ventured to

Rome, and was favourably received by Gregory, who assigned him a pension, and treated him with distinction. Hopeless, apparently, of any reformation; disappointed with that which was on its trial; worn out with years and sorrows; in the power of his enemies; he published a recantation of his works, as abounding in heresies, and injurious to the Roman Pontiff. At least this is the Roman accredited story: and certainly there is a printed book, in which *M.A. de Dominis sui reditus ex Anglia consilium exponit;* and it came *ex typographiâ Rev. Cameræ Apostolicæ*, MDCXXIII. All I can say is,—that the end of the story does not well agree with the beginning; that De Dominis's style was marvellously improved in the interval between his *De Republicâ* and his *Concilium Reditus;* that the latter book was very necessary for Rome; that the Jesuits had a good many practised pens; and that the archbishop did not live to disown the work.

Gregory XV died July 8, 1623. Urban VIII discontinued the pension of De Dominis. "Easier that,"—so, or to the same effect spoke the ex-prelate, "than to answer my *De Republicâ Ecclesiasticâ.*" His reward was a cell in the Castle of S. Angelo, and a process in the Inquisition. This was still unfinished when the report went through Rome that the imprisoned archbishop was dangerously ill. He received the sacraments of the church with great devotion, and then went to a higher tribunal than that of the Holy Office, and I assuredly trust, to a more merciful sentence. Europe believed him poisoned; four of the Pope's physicians declared that he was not. Italian poisoning being so unheard-of a thing, and the testimony of the witnesses so perfectly disinterested, let us give the Jesuits the benefit of the doubt. At all events,

> This surely yet
> Might have been granted him,—one sepulchre
> Beside the sepulchres of his forefathers.

But no. The Inquisition finished the cause, declared him a relapsed heretic, and burnt his corpse with great solemnity in the *Campo di Fiora*.

And first a few words as to the general outline of the city. Spalato may be described as a parallelogram —or rather double square—the larger side to the sea. One of these squares, that namely to the south, is comprised within the walls of the palace of Diocletian. Of this, the seaward gate is called the Porta Argentea; that to the east, the Aenea; that to the west, the Ferrea; that to the landward, the Aurea. The whole of this part of the city is so blocked up with mean alleys, staircase streets, and huddled lanes, that you are perfectly amazed when you at length enter the Peristylium, the open hall of granite columns. To your left is the Cathedral, once the great Temple of Jupiter; to your right, the church of S. Giovanni or the Baptistery, once the Temple of Æsculapius. Beyond this, you *did* pass through the Porticus, of the Corinthian order; then the Vestibulum; then the Atrium; then the Cryptoporticus; the last was 517 English feet in length, and must have commanded a most noble view of the Adriatic.

Let us commence in the Peristylium, now the Piazza del Duomo. On each side are seven Corinthian arches, which, exceedingly stilted, spring immediately from the capitals. The intercolumniations are not the same.

The three first	8ft.	9in.
4th	8	8¼
5th	10	4*
6th	9	10
7th	9	4

At the further end of the Piazza is a flight of steps to the Porticus; the latter has four Corinthian pillars, but there is a flat entablature, except for the one central arch of entrance. Let us enter the Cathedral.

"Thou hast conquered, O Galilæan!" This perfectly plain octagonal nave was formerly the great temple. It is the darkest, plainest church I ever saw,—an opening or two for light, and that is all the change made,—there really is nothing to describe. There was originally a portico, taken down when the tower was added. The interior entablatures are of the worst and heaviest taste; the sculptures of the frieze,—Cupids riding, or in chariots,—lions, bears, stags, are equally barbarous. Still, the dome, which is of brick-work, is ingenious; it consists, as it has well been said, "of a succession of small arches, one standing scalewise on the other, till they reach the upper or central part, where they are succeeded by concentric circles, as in ordinary cupolas." The height is said to be 78ft. 4in. The interior is in a disgraceful state.

Cathedral of Spalato.

The choir is square ended, much modernised; so as

* This opens to the temple staircase.

to render it impossible to guess at the original date. I should have said, that the stalls and synthronus, erected by De Dominis, were earlier; they are at least very archaic. The famous altar angels, also his device, the usual lion of the place, seem to me childish enough. They are of wood, and appear to be supporting an immense weight, till one finds that there are concealed iron-braces.

The reader will observe that I could not summon sufficient classical enthusiasm to be struck with the Cathedral in itself. But its campanile, of 173 feet in height, is one of the noblest erections of the kind that I ever yet saw. It was built by Nicolas Tevardi, a common mason of Spalato, in 1360 :. square, of five stages, with a later octagonal head; the tradition is that the latter supplied the place of two stages overthrown in a storm. No words can give an idea of the exquisite system of panel-shafting from apex to lowest stage; the shafts, usually speaking, circular; with square base, and Corinthianising caps. The lower stage, which I do not reckon in the six, is of solid masonry, only pierced by the ascent to the door. A good many of the shafts and capitals used came from the ruins of Salona, the bishopric, to the destruction of which Spalato succeeded.

By the entrance of the Cathedral is a red granite sphinx; one of two removed from the Porticus to the Temple when it was taken down. Over the door is a kind of high tomb to Margaret, daughter of Bela IV, who died in 1241, at Clissa, and with whom her sister Catherine is also buried. I also copied the following :-

  Heus tu qui transis, parumper sta.
  Johannes Fabiani Spalatensis fui,

ubi gloriam nactus sprevi et innocentiam colui. Pro me,
Viator optime 7 vale, 7 ave.

Is the latter clause a singular parody of a classical epitaph ?—or is the *vale* a mistake of the engraver for *Pater* ?

I cannot better describe the Baptistery than in the words of Sir Gardiner Wilkinson.

"About 115 feet from the opposite side of the court, and facing the Temple of Jupiter, is that of Esculapius. It stands at the upper end of a *Temenos*, or sacred inclosure, 100 feet broad and 165 long. A similar *Temenos* inclosed the other Temple; and it is probable they were both planted with trees. The interior of the cella, though simple, is ornamented with a rich projecting cornice, and carved lacunaria in its vaulted stone ceiling, which continues in a perfect state of preservation, and is a curious specimen of an ancient roof. The cornice and frieze, of the exterior, are also well preserved, particularly at the back. The bas-reliefs of the frieze represent Cupids plucking grapes, amidst trees and vases, and lions and leopards resting their paws on vases; from which this temple might seem rather to have belonged to Bacchus than to the God of medicine. But, considering how much Esculapius was honoured in the country, it is not surprising that Diocletian should dedicate one of the temples to him. So esteemed, indeed, was this deity by the Romans, that, during the great plague (A.U.C. 462), they sent to Greece, and brought away his statue, in the form of a serpent, from Epidaurus, to stay the calamity.*

* Valer. Max. lib. i. c. 8.

"Two sarcophagi have been placed in the area before the door, which were brought from Salona; on one is represented a spirited boar hunt, the other is of no interest.

"This temple, converted into a baptistery, has been dedicated to S. John; and it is to their consecration to religious purposes by the Christians, that both these ancient sanctuaries are indebted for their preservation. The steeple, that formerly disfigured the temple of Esculapius, has been taken down; and the removal of the houses, that conceal the back part, would be a still greater improvement."

Our next business was to walk round the walls of the palace, so far as they are perfect. The dimensions are these: there being a square tower at each extremity which is not included in the measurement as here given, from Adams:

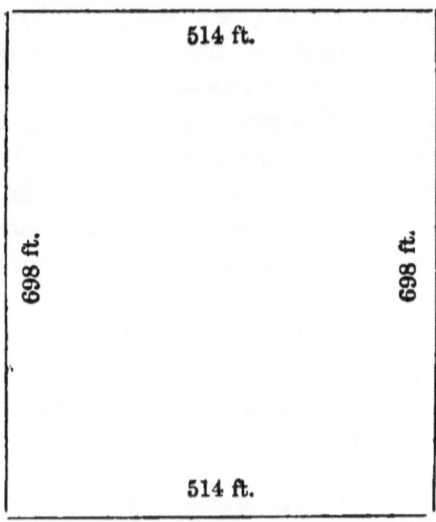

The *Porta Œnea* is utterly destroyed; there are small remains of the *Porta Argentea*, and the *Porta Ferrea*; but the *Porta Aurea* is in beautiful preservation, though the earth has been much heaped up against it. In the lower part is a gateway of very rich mouldings. Above this, a series of seven arches, once supported on porphyry columns, carried away by those barbarous depredators, the Venetians. I may now speak of the churches:

Santa Chiara by the Porta Argentea, I saw by night when lighting up for a congregation. It was originally middle-pointed, though now much modernised, with a good deal of "classic" enrichment. On the south side are cloisters of the same date, of small dimensions, but elegant. The tower seems a poor imitation of the cathedral. Spalato S. Chiara.

S. Pasquale. Also a modernized church: crammed full, when I saw it, of a congregation, at the exhibition of some relic. Spalato S. Pasquale.
This was kissed by each in turn, passing before the high altar, where it was held by the arch priest; in the meantime vernacular hymns were sung by the choir; we visited *S. John Baptist*, and *S. Dominic*, which have nothing of interest; in *S. Peter's*, here called *S. Pierro*, I copied the following:

> Joannes de Manciniis, Mil. Hieros. S. Sap.
> Canon. Archip. Spalatens. et hujus ecclesiæ
> Rector, præ vetustate demolitam
> ad fidelium commoda instauravit, et exornavit.
> MDCXCVI.

It has a pretty little campanile with three bells; but the edifice itself is disgraced with the semicircular stable windows that here are so common.

From Spalato, though not at our first stay in that city, we paid a visit to the adjacent island of Bua. *Bavus*, the Boas of Ammian, was a not unusual place of exile under the Lower empire. It is manifestly a continuation of the promontory on which Spalato itself stands; and, at its northern extremity, approaches within five hundred yards of the littoral to which it is actually joined by Trau (that Trau of which I spoke not long since as the see of Andreucci). That we failed to visit this, the ancient Tragurium, was our only serious disappointment in our Dalmatian tour.

Sailing out of the harbour, we coasted the eastern side of the peninsula, which is called Mount Marianna: here is the cemetery. Double that, to our right opened the whole sketch of the littoral along the canal of Bua. It is the loveliest coast scenery of Dalmatia, and goes by the name of the Castelli; from the fact that so many of the Venetian nobility were glad to establish their families, and to erect their castles in this earthly Paradise. Thus we have Castelsuçuraz, Castelabbadessa, Castelcambio, Castelvetturi, &c. Then we stood across the little strait, and in two hours from leaving Spalato landed at a little long quay in Bua, an olive yard rising abruptly above it. There were a few boats lying at anchor here, each with four gratellas, two at either end, to hold lights for the night fishery of Sardines.

We pursued our way up the olive yard, and then

through a deep stony lane. An old peasant met us with the salutation (south of Spalato so all but universal) *Hvalien Isus:* "JESUS be praised!" You reply: *Vazda:* "for ever," or, *Vazda buddi i Maria:* "for ever be He, and also Mary!" And still ascending, we came out on a little bit of table land, where stands the small church of *S. George Zlatinski*. It has square-ended chancel, nave, south sacristy, campanile. The whole is very rude, and of Romanesque date. Two brackets at east end, like early Romanesque above—a square aumbrye to the north of the chancel, and a very low circular chancel arch. The sacristy was once a chapel; it has a west door, with a rather curious first pointed benatura. The woman from whom we got the keys (and she seemed miserably poor), shook her head at paper, looked doubtful at silver, but accepted copper with avidity. The view from the churchyard, stretching on one side to Trau, whose towers you can see as at the end of a deep bay, along the Castelli opposite—further on to Point Marianna, the island rises too high on the other side to allow of a view to the open Adriatic. In the churchyard is a slab of the fifteenth century, showing the same custom of representing the profession of the deceased which prevailed among ourselves. Here was the *Piperata*, pruning hook, of exactly the same shape that is employed now.

Bua Zlatinski.

In returning to our boat, I saw a pretty, little ball of crisp, green foliage, something like an "everlasting," and gathered it. Directly my fingers became violently inflamed,—the pain was at least equal to that of a wasp sting, and I could even feel shooting pains all up my arm for some time. It was, I found, the bud of a particular kind of nettle, for which Bua is famous.

Chapter IX.

MACARSKA, CURZOLA, CATTARO.

EARLY in the morning after we had left Spalato, we lay to off Macarska. A very grand view: bleak snow-capped mountains rising precipitously behind; so pure and clear in the unclouded and, as yet, chilly May morning. Close at hand, pleasant little gardens running down almost to the beach; the white houses of the little city contrasting well with the scattered groves of fir or cypress; the Venetian towers here and there; and the life and business of the country quay.

The single hour that we had for visiting this place was amply enough. Its ecclesiastical history will appear elsewhere; here it may suffice to say that it always maintained its independence as a separate republic under Venetian protection. And this was not a mere form of words; Venice had very little real power here, and the Lion nowhere appears on the public edifices. A grove of trees is still shown, which formed the city town hall.

The *Concathedral*, so called from the union of the see with that of Spalato, is a plain, long, modern building,—the tower on the north side; but without any object of interest. To the south of, and beyond, the town is the Convent

<small>Macarska Concathedral.</small>

of the Assumption, or of S. Antonio, a Franciscan house; the church modern; a tall Venetian tower; cinque-cento cloisters. The convent stands in a grove of firs, itself occupying part of a little green; the mountains tower up close behind. This is one of the loveliest situations I ever saw a religious house occupy.

As you again steam along the coast, the littoral puts on its loveliest features. Village after village of ravishing beauty; merry songs and voices from olive-yard and vineyard; the ploughing oxen; the goatherd's pipe; the glorious mountains looking down upon and solemnising all. To our right, we are nearing the long thin island of Lésina — "the awl" — so called from its shape; in Illyrian *Far*. It approaches us almost at right angles; but I shall leave what I have to say of it till hereafter, when we shall visit its capital.

We pass between the mainland and the point, by S. George's Channel, and almost reverse our late course, along the other side of the island. A glance at the map will shew the curious position of the littoral, Lésina, and the long promontory of Sabbion-cello. Till lately we have been running south-east, the littoral to our left, Lésina to our right; now we are running north-west, Lesina to our right, the littoral only in view, Sabbioncello to our left, till we can double the point of the latter. In about an hour our course changes; we pass within a hundred yards of the utmost point of that quaint peninsula; go round it; and now find ourselves in a river lake between Sabbioncello and Curzola. And now, on the latter island, I see a quaint mediæval, walled town, boldly projecting into the sea; the waves licking the feet of the very battlements. This is Curzola. We shut off our steam, and cast anchor. I jump into the boat with the certainty that this is, of a verity, new ecclesiological ground.

There is not a street in the little town through which any vehicle could pass; neither could the gates admit the entrance of such a thing. It is a city of alleys and staircases: but *so* picturesque! First to *S. Michael*: a very small church, of apparently first-pointed date, now modernized. Square-ended chancel: dome: very small nave. Nothing especially worthy of notice save the pulpit, which projects from the north wall; and is supported on four circular voluted shafts, with square flowered caps, and is richly moulded. As we pass up the street, we are shown a ring, which in mediæval times gave to him that was so happy as to grasp it, the privilege of asylum. Next to the *ci-devant Cathedral*—a very curious building. Circular apse: choir: nave: two north aisles, one south aisle, to choir and nave: tower at north west. The whole first-pointed.

<small>Curzola S. Michael.</small>

<small>Curzola Cathedral.</small>

The altar stands in the chord of the apse; the stalls and bishop's throne are of cinque-cento work. The choir and nave together have five bays: arches pointed, and quite plain. Piers circular, on square base, and with Corinthianising caps. In the triforum are two openings over each bay: the two separated by a circular shaft with square flowered caps and square base. The clerestory had, *apparently*, one lancet to each bay, but is now modernized. The south aisle is apsidal; the apse now blocked by an altar. On the south side, high up, is a cinque-cento recessed monument to a Bishop of Curzola, Vincent Cossovich. The effigy is lying on one side. To the north of north aisle is an irregular opening, but towards the east by two-and-a-half arches to the sacristy, to which also is a singularly rich door: square-headed trefoiled: the cusps being formed by angels with musical instruments; above very rich work with IHS and the Resurrection in the tympanum. By this door is a cinque-cento benatura. The sacristy itself has two bays from north to south—the windows were accordingly lancets. The second north aisle has two-and-a-half narrow bays. Two lancets to the north, two to the west; the east end is blocked. Here they profess to show a Titian. The tower, at the north-west, has a very rich western door, of two voluted orders, and a canonized bishop in the tympanum. The west window of the nave is a fine rose of sixteen leaves.

This is a very instructive church; and coming in so romantically situated a city, and utterly unexpected, it delighted us extremely. We then saw *All Saints*. This is modernized; but has some curious things.

<small>Curzola All Saints.</small>

The baldachin seems of the thirteenth century. The shafts are circular with Corinthianizing caps; the dome pierced with quatrefoils; at each angle a pinnacle. A staircase in the north leads to what was once a Greek church, though now deserted. Several old Greek pictures remain in a state of decay.

Curzola is the *Corcyra Nigra* of the ancients, so

called from its dark pine woods. They now supply Lloyd's arsenal, and make the island one of the loveliest of the Adriatic group.

On board again. For some distance yet we run between Sabbioncello and Curzola; then a break to our right; and we near, and begin to run along, *Meleda*.

Now I must confess that, till our present tour, I had always, notwithstanding the confessed difficulties attaching to that hypothesis, believed the Melita of the Acts of the Apostles to be *Malta*. It is, of course, a subject which has been deeply studied in the monasteries of these islands; and, after examining the authorities recommended to me by some of their religious, I am bound to express my entire certainty that Melita is Meleda. If it be thought presumptuous in me—a clergyman—to contradict such authorities as Admiral Penrose and Mr. Smith, I must observe that every Adriatic naval authority is on my side. I will briefly state the argument:

The plain facts, which make for me, are these:—

1. The ship was driven "up and down in Adria." *It is said* that the sea between Malta and Crete was anciently called Adria. Let us first have a proof of this; as yet I have seen none, except where the word is used vaguely, *e.g.* as one might now say;—I went from Trieste by the Adriatic to Malta;—which would not mean that the Adriatic *reached* to Malta.

2. There are no serpents in Malta; they abound in Meleda.

3. The same of wood.

4. The sailors must have known Malta; yet," when it was day, they knew NOT the land."

5. I lay no great stress on the "barbarous people," yet the expression is singular if employed of the Maltese.

6. There is *no creek* in Malta such as described. The Maltese hypothesis make the sailors take the Salmonetta strait for a creek. In Meleda, S. Paul's Bay answers precisely.

7. Any Maltese tradition may be repulsed by the universal tradition of the Adriatic in favour of Meleda.

Let us follow the ship from Clauda.

The wind was then blowing—as it is agreed—E.N.E. Under the lea of Clauda they had smooth water for some twelve miles, and employed themselves in making all snug: that is, after lowering the mainyard, and perhaps setting a small storm-sail, they hove the ship to on the starboard tack. Mr. Smith calculates the drift to be a mile, or a mile and a half, an hour, which on the fourteenth night would make Malta.

I first quote Admiral Penrose:

"To have drifted up the Adriatic, to the island of Meleda, in the requisite course, and to have passed so many islands would, humanly speaking, have been impossible. The distance from Clauda to that Meleda is not less than 780 geographical miles.

Now observe:

1. The distance to Meleda is little more than 620 miles. I cannot but imagine the Admiral to have thought that *Melada*, quite in the north of the Adriatic group, was meant. That *is* about 780 miles from Malta; that *would* involve a curve to get to it. But suppose

2. That, when the ship was in 22° east longitude

35° north latitude, the wind shifted, *as it so often does*, to E.S.E. The course would be then directly straight to Meleda,—no island approaching the line—S. Paul's Bay, the creek so exactly answering the description, would be the first land they could make.

3. On this hypothesis, there was not *one single* island, instead of the Admiral's "so many," to pass.

Whatever may be thought on the whole, any reader may convince himself that from Clauda to Meleda there is nothing like 780 miles; and that no curve was necessary to enable the ship to reach it,—the southernmost of all the Adriatic group. I cannot, I repeat, but believe that the Admiral was thinking of Melada.

We had time, as we ran along the pretty, though rather monotonous island, to discuss this and the like subjects; though S. Paul's cove lies on the exterior side, we cheered ourselves with the hope of seeing it on our return. A storm came on; and a rainbow spanned the narrow strait from Meleda to Gravosa;—the spotless wing of the sea-bird dipped sometimes for a moment in its prismatic glory. We cast anchor in the bay of Gravosa, two miles from Ragusa, late in the afternoon; and immediately made the best of our way to the city. I will not now describe it; but will reserve it for our return, when we passed a longer time here. On this occasion we only remained the night.

We left Gravosa again at seven in the morning. The coast scenery was at first uninteresting; but the moment the point was doubled, and we entered the long winding, mountain-locked "*Canal*" of Cattaro, we were overwhelmed with the sublime loveliness of this heavenly fiord. Now a noble river; now a calm lake; now a narrow sea; it opens at length into the final reach, and Cattaro reposes at the further end. The huge mountains that mirror themselves so lovingly on the calm waters; the venerable old woods; olive-yards and vineyards; white cottages peeping out from the laurel groves; monasteries shrouded in cypress trees; red May-bushes sending out their fragrance from hill side or towering promontory; the distant farm; the village, with its church, lining the far-off shore; the glorious hues of the crags and such a sky as is reflected nowhere save in the Adriatic! That two hours' voyage, from the Bocca to Cattaro, must be, I really believe, summing its elements of beauty in one, unrivalled in Europe. At Perasto, where the last reach opens, the steamer calls:—the little town stands on the Canal as in the bifurcation of a **Y**; the stem leads seaward; the left arm winds away into, and is lost in, Monte Crassene; the right runs up to Cattaro.

That verily *is* a city of beauty! The mountains soar precipitously from the very beach; the town rises with them; and, when the "lamb-clouds" are at an average height, the exterior walls, on the Albanian side, peer far above them. This, too, is one of those places one dreams of; such steep, narrow alleys; houses almost touching each other in the upper storey; staircased streets. We entered the seagate, in front of which is a pretty grove, boulevard-like; and began to make inquiries for lodgings, for professed hotel there is none. Having secured two rooms, empty of furniture but swarming with very unnecessary tenants, we left Dundich to purchase what provisions were needful, and proceeded to the *Cathedral*,—a very interesting and instructive building. It stands in a little *place*, almost the only flat piece of ground, in the centre of the city.

<small>Cattaro Cathedral.</small>

It consists of
    Apse, with adjacent north chapel,
    Choir, with aisles,
    Nave, with aisles,
    Two western towers.

The whole is late Romanesque. The apse is circular, with remains of the original synthronus; the altar stands in the centre of the chord. At the east end are three circular-headed lights, with circular shafts, and square caps.

The altar is under a late third-pointed baldachin; shafts octagonal; octagonal, on square, base; rudely flowered square caps, supporting a richly flowered flat architrave; above which rises a cinque-cento octagonal canopy.

At the south-east of the apse, high up in the wall, is an episcopal monument like that at Curzola. The effigy lies quite on one side; the hands are crossed; the niche is very high;—the Bishop wears a cope,—and in the upper part of his Pastoral Staff is a Holy Lamb. There is an inscription in hexameters, so carelessly (to all appearance) engraved at first, and so much mutilated, as not to be worth transcription. The last line is:—

Ano Dni. MDXXXII. de X. mens. Novembr.

Below this, on the floor, is an incised slab of another Prelate.

To the north of the apse is a door which communicates with the sacristy,—a small chapel parallel with the church. The vaulting is pointed; all else modernised.

The choir of the Cathedral consists of one bay, that is, two arches; for, throughout the building, each couple of arches are contained under an external arch. This external arch forms the vaulting; the two interior arches are very narrow,—all round-headed. The shaft circular; square base; square Corinthianizing cap: very good and solemn. The vaulting of the bay simply cross, with broad, flat, square-edged mouldings. The stalls are poor and modern; not returned.

The south aisle of the choir has *now* a square East end; but the apse arch remains, and is bold and good. On the south side is a circular-headed light, *now* trefoiled. The north aisle is much the same as the south, excepting this window.

The nave consists of two bays (= four arches) like the choir. The piers very massy, and square; simple cross-vaulting to each bay; the clerestory has one circular-headed light to each *arch*. Then, beyond, one arch is set a little further back on each side:—was this intended for a proposed tower, never built? The south aisle has one circular-headed window, now trefoiled in each bay. This may remind us of those in the Cathedral of Pola. At the north-west end of the north aisle is a modern baptistery; and from this a flight of twenty steps leads into the chapter-house, which appears to have been taken out of a chapel. Here is a perfect collection of chapter records, since the year 1436; the hasty glance I was able to give showed me how many curious things might be gleaned from it. For example:

> Hoc anno, die xx mens. Novembris, erat ventus valde furens: et evertit omnes arbores, et quasdam domos, et crucem, quæ in septentrionali parte Cathedralis posita erat.
> Quocirca statutum est, ut singulis annis omnes in urbe campanæ hac in nocte pulsentur.

This joins on the north side to what was the Episcopal Palace.

There is a curious Romanesque barrel-vaulted porch. On the left hand, as you enter, a singular sarcophagus. Over it:

> Sarcophagum
> Conjugum nobilissimorum,
> qui, anno a Christo Nato DCCCIX,
> ecclesiæ S. Mariæ, infuario jam pridem carenti
> D. Tryphonis a mercatoribus Ven: emptis exuviis
> templum primo hic ædificaverunt
> Quum ejus ambitus novissime strueretur
> hic prope sub foramine detectæ, effossæque
> v. non. April. A.S. MDCCCXI.

On the north wall is this inscription, evidently coeval with the church; but so worn as to be almost illegible. The interest which our attempts to decypher it occasioned, showed how very little attention is paid to archæology at Cattaro.

> + Sum pulvis factus, pulvis de pulvere tractus.
> Sergius sum Episcopus, Leonis cujusdam filii
> Qui cum starem corpus sustinui includi in hoc tumulo
> Omnes qui aspicitis, orate pro nostris contagiis sedulo.
> Dominum deprecate, cujus discipulus fuit * * mille * * nono

The east end, as I have said, was triapsidal; this is manifest enough in the exterior, though the northern apse has perished. The southern apse, circular, has three bays, divided by plain flat Romanesque pilaster-buttresses; each bay panelled in two nebuly arches; in the central bay is one round-headed light, now blocked.

The central apse is, in like manner, divided into three bays; each having four nebuly arches. The central bay has a large round-headed window, with circular shafts, and square caps. Above this, are two quatrefoiled circles. The whole is a very curious example of an early Romanesque east end.

The western façade consists of two seventeenth century towers, connected by a great circular arch; forming, beneath it, a porch, flanked on each side by one of the towers. Above this arch is a passage with balusters,—I suppose that the Bishop might thence bless the people assembled in the great square, which it overlooks. The west window of the nave, which appears above this, is a rose of sixteen trefoiled lights.

North-west of the Cathedral is the curious little church of *S. Luke*, an early Romanesque structure.

<small>Cattaro.
S. Luke.</small> It consists of apse, central dome, and western narthex. The apse is circular; the apse arch plain, round. The dome rises from a square external structure on four pointed Romanesque arches. Outside, the church is square, with the addition of the apse; and, under a lean-to, to the north, the apsidal chapel of S. Spiridion, which has no windows. The apse of S. Luke is externally

divided into three panels by flat pilaster-buttresses; the central division has two round-headed adjacent lights; shafts, circular; circular base, square caps. The south side of the square has one clerestory window terminating a pilaster-buttress, something like those at Clymping, Sussex. The western façade has, under one great circular arch of construction, two adjacent Romanesque lights under one arch. Below this, a circular-headed door, with well-moulded jambs. The north side is much as the south. In the dome, toward each cardinal point, is a very narrow, round-headed, lancet. The dome terminates in a pyramidal head. This church belongs to the Eastern rite. The Iconostasis appears of the seventeenth century.

We here made the acquaintance of the Archimandrite, Irenæus Popovitch, who, as I have already said, is Pro-Vicar of the Bishop in the southern part of his diocese. He has two priests under him: they seem well-informed men, and certainly of a superior stamp to the general run of their Latin brethren. They introduced us to the Slavonic reading-room, where they are endeavouring to get a few periodicals together, devoted to the interests of the Eastern Church; and presented us with a recently-published octavo, in handsome Cyrillic type,—" Istorie Tsrne Gore: napesao D. Milakovitch:" Zara, 1856, (A history of Montenegro),—to which I shall have occasion to refer again.

I very much regret that the accidental loss of my notes of the very curious Romanesque *Collegiata* render me unable to describe it.

We had but one day in Cattaro, and were anxious

to employ it to the best advantage. We first procured horses for Montenegro, and then an unexpected difficulty arose. Dundich's passport was *visé* for almost every European State : unhappily, Montenegro did not appear among the rest. The authorities were unpersuadable. "You must telegraph to Trieste." We did so. The answer was, "Telegraph broken somewhere in Croatia, between Zengh and Sebenico." We applied again. Still the only reply was, " Perhaps it will be mended before you start."

After seeing the churches which I have described, we took a long walk by the "canal,"—assuredly the most glorious firth-scenery I have ever seen. Norway, I imagine, may, in height of mountains and grandeur of composition, be equal to it; but southern colouring and southern vegetation, and the blue of the Adriatic, render the scene inimitable. I wonder that Cattaro is not better known. Even Wilkinson seems to me vastly to underrate its beauties. A very fair road skirts the eastern side of the firth; snow-capped mountains towered beyond, and be-hither, the calm gulf; white cottages peeped out from their luxuriance of blossom —apple, pear, cherry, pumpkin, plum; vines trellised the garden alley-walk; oliveyards and vineyards, maize and wheat, clothed the lower slopes; seared and seamed rocks, here and there, cropped out from the rank vegetation; white-sailed boats tacked or bounded merrily before the wind; mountain-convents rang out for vespers; in scattered nooks a boat-house was reflected in the blue firth. And so we passed on till we came to Dobrota, the little village that stands at the head of the first reach, the bay here opening out in three ramifications. The white church stands well, overhanging a plateau of some 300 feet above the level of the sea: it is, unhappily, modern. Here we hired a boat, crossed the "canal," and walked back on the other side, skirting the head of the lake, and entering the fortifications by a narrow and curious, but most fetid, postern at twilight.

Our quarters, which, as I have said, were in a private house, were comfortless and bare, devoid of everything but vermin. They sheltered us, however, from a tremendous thunder-storm which burst on the mountains immediately over our heads that night.

Before I say anything of Montenegro, I will offer a few observations on the ecclesiastical condition of Dalmatia.

Chapter X.

ECCLESIASTICAL DALMATIA.

In the present chapter I propose to give a brief sketch of the organization of the Church, both Latin and Greek, in Dalmatia. My materials are taken, partly from private information, partly from the "Schematismi," published for the Greek Province, and for most of the Latin dioceses, by the brothers Battara, of Zara,—the best publishing house south of Trieste.

The Latin Province has Zara for its metropolis, with a diocesan population of 51,214 souls. The regular clergy are 41, the secular 216; the parishes and chapelries 88. The Cathedral of Zara, and the Collegiate church in the Island of Pago, are the two most important ecclesiastical establishments. There are two diocesan seminaries, the one for Latin, the other for Illyrian, priests;—the latter called after the great and good Archbishop Vincent Zmaievich, its founder. (He sat from 1713 to 1746.) The first Bishop, of whom the ecclesiastical records of the province tell, was S. Felix, about 380: the first Archbishop was Lampridius de Gallelis, raised to that dignity in A.D. 1146. The present Archbishop, Joseph Godeassi, is the fifty-fifth in succession.

Next comes the bishopric of Spalato and Macarska: its Cathedral in the former, its *Concathedral* in the latter, city. Both will be described hereafter. Spalato, which, under the name of Salona, figures as a bishopric as early as 500, was afterwards raised to Archiepiscopal dignity, and again degraded to simple diocesan dignity in 1830. In that year Macarska, up to that time an independent diocese, was united to its more illustrious sister. I noticed, in the almanac of the united dioceses, one or two singular observances. Thus, on the 19th of January, after the Angelus, and early on the morning of the 20th, all the bells are to be rung, in consequence of a destructive hurricane which, some 300 years ago, is said to have uprooted every single tree in the diocese of Spalato. From the Feast of S. Mark to that of S. Luke, the Collect "Ad repellendas tempestates," is to be said daily, with reference to the terrible Bora, of which I have already spoken. S. Domnius, first Bishop of Salona, is principal patron of the diocese. His festival is on the 10th of May, and its octave is a season of daily merrymaking. S. John Baptist has no vigil, because another celebrated prelate of Salona, S. Venantius, is commemorated on that day. On the Nativity of S. Mary a splendid procession takes place in Spalato, in commemoration of the cessation, in that city, of the fearful plague of 1516. There are daily suffrages of their respective Saints in the Cathedral church of S. Domnius, S. Anastasius, and S. Jerome. The united diocese contains 117,905 souls, 141 churches and chapels, 214 secular, 29 regular, priests.

Next comes Ragusa. It contains 71 churches and chapels, 39 regular, 97 secular, priests; 55,175 souls. This see, once raised to Archiepiscopal dignity, was again reduced to a simple bishopric in 1830.

After this comes Lesina. The official title of the Prelate is *Pharensis*—or, rather, *Pharensis et Bractensis*—Pharos being the ancient name of Lesina, and Brazza forming so important a part of the diocese. It contains 41 churches and chapels; 10 regular, and 71 secular, priests; 35,146 souls. This embraces, also, the diocese of Curzola, suppressed in 1830.

Sebenico follows. It is formed of three dioceses:—

1. Knin (Lat. Thinniensis). This see was founded by Cresimir IV, King of Croatia, in 1050; and fifty-eight prelates governed it till 1714, when it was lost by the Venetians to the Turks. The Emperor, as King of Hungary, continued to name a titular bishop, as, I believe, he does to this day. In 1768, the city was recaptured, and it was intended to re-establish the diocese; but difficulties intervened; and it was first informally, and then actually, united to the Diocese of Sebenico.

2. Scardona. This see existed at least as early as 580, and possessed its own Bishops till October 8, 1813. It was then governed by Vicars-General till 1830, when it was definitively united to Sebenico.

3. Sebenico. The see was founded in 1279, and has possessed several eminent prelates. Girolamo Saorniano distinguished himself at Trent, and in 1564 convoked his first Diocesan Synod. Vincenzo da Brescia (1599—1627) held seven. Giovanni Petani, was the most learned Illyrian scholar of his day, and the first President of the Zmaievich Seminary at Zara. The united dioceses contain 52 churches and chapels, 34 secular, 54 regular, priests, and 69,442 souls. This is the only Dalmatian see in which the

regulars outnumber the seculars. This arises from the number of the places where a religious house—when there was constant war with the Turks—might safely be founded. I have before me a list of the dedications of all the churches in the diocese. The ecclesiologist may be interested by a tabular view of it:

S. Mary	. . . 19	The Holy Ghost	3	The Name of Jesus	2
S. George	. . 8	S. Elias . . .	3	All Saints . . .	2
S. John Baptist	. 7	S. Katherine . .	3	S. James . . .	2
S. Antony	. . 6	S. Peter . . .	3	S. Jerome . . .	2
S. Michael	. . 6	S. Stephen . .	3		
S. Nicolas	. . 5				
S. Mark	. . . 4				

And these one each:—S. Anne, S. Cross, S. Daniel, S. Francis, S. Gregory, S. John Ursini, S. Margaret, S. Martin, S. Mary Magdalene, SS. Peter and Paul, SS. Philip and James, S. Roque, SS. Roque and Bartholomew, S. Silvester, S. Thomas.

One may notice in these dedications a good deal of the influence of the Eastern Church. The favourite Saints, George and John Baptist, take the lead of all others; and the rare dedication of S. Katherine and the almost unknown one of S. Elias, here stand high.

Lastly, there is the Diocese of Cattaro. This contains 24 churches and chapels, 43 secular, 22 regular, priests; 20,164 souls.

The whole province of Dalmatia, then, contains:— 417 churches and chapels, 195 regular, 683 secular, priests; 487,042 souls.

I will now speak of the Eastern Church. It may not be uninteresting to the reader to have some information with respect to its present status in the Austrian dominions generally; the rather that the names of its prelates are constantly occurring in the political negotiations now going on in Hungary.

The Austro-Oriental Church, then, numbering about 4,000,000 of souls, is subject to, as its supreme earthly head, the Patriarch of Servia, Metropolitan of Carlovitz. His official title—if the reader is fond of long words—is,—

Ego Sviatost Prevoskhodetelnieeshie e Vuisokodostoenieeshie Joseph Raiatchietch.

Under this dignitary are,—

1. Bishop of Karlstadt; Peter Joannovitch. Resides at Plashk.
2. Bishop of the Bukovine; Eugenius Chakman. Resides at Tchernovitz.
3. Bishop of Bats; Plato Athanaskovitch.
4.   „   Pakrats; Stephen Kragouevitch.
5.   „   Transylvania; Andrew Shaguna. Resides at Hermannstadt.
6. Bishop of Temesvar; Samuel Masherevitch.
7.   „   Vershatz; Emilian Kengelats.
8.   „   Bude; Arsenius Stoekovitch.
9.   „   Arad; Procopius Ivatzkovitch.
10.   „   Dalmatia; Stephen Knezevitch.

It was not till the end of the seventeenth century that the Eastern Church had a Bishop for the Venetian States. Then Meletius, Metropolitan of Philadelphia, taking refuge from the savage persecutions of the Turks, settled at Venice. The succession has been this:—

2. Nicodemus Bousovitch, calling himself Bishop of Sebenico, +1690.
3. Sabbatius.
4. Stephen Liobiebratitch; 'settled at Cattaro, +1718.
5. Simeon Kontsaveritch, with the title of Bishop of Carniola and Dalmatia; +1750.

6. Sophronius Kutovalle, ex-Metropolitan of Philadelphia, with two ex-Archbishops; +1790. Vacant till 1810.
7. Benedict Kralevitch, at Zara; +1829. Governed the last seven years by an ex-Archbishop.
8. Joseph Raiatchietch, now Patriarch, till 1834.
9. Panteleemon Jevkovitch; +1835. Vacant till 1844.
10. Hierotheus Madebasitch; +1853.
11. Stephen Knezevitch, the present Bishop, who, like his immediate predecessors, resides at Zara.

I have already said that education is on a very creditable scale in both Churches. Some of the Latin books of religion I will here mention.

One is everywhere struck by the appearance of the same little volume in all but the meanest cottages. It is what Dr. Watts's Hymns are to England, or Father Catz to Holland. It is called, "Muka Gospodina nascega Isukarsta e plac Matera Njegove,"— The Passion of our Lord Jesus Christ, and the Complaint of His Mother. It is a poem written dialogue-wise between our Lord, His Mother, and others present at the Passion; and from the easy flow of its rhythm, the elegance of its language, and its own worth, has become marvellously popular. It was composed by a Franciscan, Peter Knezevitch, and published in 1752. He died about 1770. Illyrian is admirably adapted for double rhymes; it has a sweetness about it, united with a strength, which perhaps are not found in any other European tongue. Here is a specimen :—

Gospe.	Our Lady.
A vidifli, Sinko mili,	Ah, beholdest thou, Son dear,
Kako tvoja Majka cvili?	How Thy Mother mourns?
Obrazdise, i vidime	—He turns, and sees me,
I s' pogledom utifime.	And with His presence calm me, &c., &c.

Ter tolije zate odicha?
(Dasam martv', ah kamo sricha)
Toli razlog koga çine
Ljudi vrutku od istine? &c.

RICI PICAOCA.	SPEECH OF THE WRITER.
Dokle Gospe naricase	While our Lady laments,
I svom Sinku govorafe,	And to her Son speaks,
Sva dovarvi po gotovu	They conduct Him already near,
Vojska dvoru Pilatovu.	With a multitude to the court of Pilate, &c., &c.

Sajde Pilat potom toga,
I videchi svezanoga:
Koja tuxba, reçe njima,
Suproch tomu od vas ima? &c.

This, then, as I have said, is *the* favourite sacred poem of Dalmatia; and though it makes small pretence to poetic diction or imagination, yet its smooth trochaic flow, and its almost Scriptural simplicity, may well endear it to the poor. I have heard it repeated in class by the schools of the larger towns, just as in England one might ask for the Evening or the Morning Hymn. And so far it stands alone. Yet Dalmatia may boast a series of Ecclesiastical poets, not easily, all things taken into consideration, to be surpassed by any other European country. Let me name a few. Marko Marulić, born at Spalato, in 1450, and who died in 1524. His versified Scripture history—for it is little more than that—is still dear to old-fashioned people, much as such books as "Law's Serious Call" might be to English Churchmen. Again, Mavro Vetranić; born in 1482, died 1576. Some of his odes or hymns, call them which you will, on Saints' Days, are extremely beautiful; a kind of antiquated "Christian Year." To these may be added his "Temptation

of Abraham," his "Passion of our LORD," and his
"Trial of Susanna." All these dramas are even
now favourites with the people. Again, the "Christiad" of Junio Palmotić, who lived from 1606 to 1657,
is a poem of no small merit. In the same measure as
the great work on the Passion, its trochaic rhymes
are alternate instead of consequent. If somewhat
more poetical, it loses more in simplicity than it gains
in ornament. Yet again; there is a beautiful Christian drama on the subject of S. Justina (though having
no connection with that glorious play of Calderon),
by Vladislav Minčetić (he died in 1666). Andrija
Vitaljić published, in 1703, at Vienna, a poetical version of the Psalms, which I have heard highly spoken
of; but I believe that the hymns, which he brought
out in 1712, and which are in great measure imitations
of those in the Roman Breviary, are still more admired.
His versions of the "Vexilla Regis," the "Stabat
Mater," the "Pange Lingua Gloriosi," are usually
employed when vernacular hymns are sung in processions or on pilgrimages. Andrija Kačić or Miočić
left a series of hymns, chiefly on the warrior-saints of
Servia and Hungary. Some of them, especially that
on S. John Capistran, are marvellously spirited; and,
I have no doubt, stirred the blood of Montenegrin or
Ragusan in their hand-to-hand conflict with the infidel,
like a trumpet. In later years, Gèrgur Čevapović
has given us a very pretty drama on the subject of
Joseph in Egypt, where we find classical metres introduced with considerable success. The Sapphics especially—if Sapphics those may be called where the
three first lines of the stanza are one syllable too short,

—are said to be much admired. But the work which, in different parts, is most usually found in Dalmatian cottages,—brought home, I suppose, by the children who are scholars in the various National Schools, just as our Christian Knowledge books abound in our English cottages,—is called " Cvit razlika mirisa duhovnoga:" that is, "The Garland of Spiritual Flowers." It contains various little devotional books of meditation and prayers, explanations of the Creeds, commentaries on our LORD's Passion, easy polemical dissertations against the faith of the Eastern Church, and a very large collection of hymns. Of these last, it is to be observed that there are probably more original hymns in the Dalmatian (Latin) Church than had been composed by any other national communion in Europe.

The only other book which seems to have a general village circulation, so to speak, among the wilder parts of the country, is, " The Art of Dying well," originally written by a Discalceate Carmelite (Joannes a Jesu Maria), and translated, in 1653, by Peter Gaudentius, then Bishop of Arbe. The language is now a little old-fashioned; but I remember, while taking refuge from a sudden shower of rain in a cottage within the Montenegrin territory, and looking at this the only volume which my temporary host possessed, that he said, " If ever I get to heaven, I shall owe it to that book." And truly it is a very excellent little treatise.

While dwelling on the subject of this people's belief, it is natural to say something of their superstitions. In Portugal, I have always been very much struck with the Lobishome of popular credence. By day, a young man or young woman; by night compelled to oam the country at full gallop as a horse. There is precisely the same belief in Dalmatia, only its object is called an Orca. Again, the Mačić is a spirit which appears in the shape of a boy surrounded with a halo of fire, and is supposed to predict the greatest good fortune for the rest of their lives to those who are so happy as to be favoured with its sight: (the reader may remember Lord Castlereagh's Vision). Nowhere is more implicit belief given to tales of vampires; and it is no uncommon thing, even at the present day, that a whole village should, for weeks together, be disturbed by the supposed apparition of a Vukožlak,—a corruption of the Greek Vrukolakes.

At the first French Revolution, it was thought a marvellous improvement to re-name the old months by titles expressive of their physical character. The Illyrian months had long anticipated such a system of denomination. Thus, January is Siecanj; that is, "the time of cutting,"—viz., cutting wood for fire. February is Vegliaça; that is, "the changeable month." March is Ojujak; that is, "of clearing,"—viz., the weeds from the corn. April is Travagn; "the month of herbs." May, still more poetically, Ivibagn,—that is, "entwining;" spoken of the twisting together of bird's nests. June, Liepahan, or Liepagn: "the beautiful month." July, Suropagn,—"sickle month." August, Kolovoz,—"the carting month." September, Ruijan,—"the red month;" referring, some say, to the change of the trees; others, to the ruddy tint of most Dalmatian wine. October is Listopad,—"leaf-fall month." November is Studeni,—"cold month." December, Prosinac, from the verb Prosinuti, "to shine;" because it is illuminated, so to speak, by our LORD's Nativity.

Chapter XI.

MONTENEGRO.

We were very anxious to pay, however hurriedly, a visit to Montenegro; which, though, shorn of its interest since the alteration of its hierarchical government, has yet sufficient difference from every other European State, to render a visit, though it may be brief, an entrance, as it were, into a perfectly novel scene.

Having hired three horses for ourselves (permission having been obtained for Dundich) and one as a sumpter animal, we rode out of Cattaro about 7 in the morning. The pavement of the city is so extremely slippery, that, to prevent accidents, our baggage was not packed till we were fairly outside the walls, in the place where the Montenegrins usually hold their market. Almost the very moment that Cattaro is left, the ascent of the mountain begins, admirably engineered by a series of zigzags, and presenting at each turn a nobler and nobler prospect,—at first, of the Canal, afterwards of the eastern coast, and, finally, of mountain-range behind mountain-range, stretching onward to the interior. This road was a work of the Austrian Government; and, though followed by the Montenegrins in ascending it, it is utterly neglected by them in the descent, when, however heavily loaded, they jump down from parapet to parapet, endeavouring merely to strike out the shortest, without any regard to the easiest, line. For the first three-quarters of an hour, the citadel of Cattaro towers high above you on the right hand; and, before you attain its elevation, you pass the small Morlacco hamlet of Spigliari. Here a road strikes off to the right, which eventually leads to Budua, and the southernmost extremity of the Austrian dominions in Turkey; but a few miles off. This hamlet contains nine houses; and there is a tradition that, should that number ever be exceeded, the place will at once be destroyed. The Austrian frontier extends some way beyond this; and the moment we pass that, the mountain-road ends. We are forced to dismount, and our horses clamber as well as they can through watercourses and over rocks; so utterly bad a road that I think Portugal could not match it.

It is almost impossible to imagine, without having seen, the marvellous effect of those mountain-ranges, tossed in the wildest confusion one behind the other, as you look to the Herzegovina and to Bosnia. It is no uncommon thing to make out fifteen or sixteen lines of mountain at once. About four hours' from Cettigne, we came on a kind of desolate plateau, where was a miserable cottage, dignified by our servant with the name of "The Hotel." It consists of one room, into which fowls, horses, and men have promiscuous entrance. The poor people that keep it belong to the Eastern Church, and there was the little icon of S. Mary, hanging in the corner of their room,—the place of honour here as in Russia. A wretched daub it was; but it received as much veneration from the Montenegrin muleteers, who were dining while we fed our beasts, as the most precious relique in the most gorgeous church could ever enjoy. Hence it is necessary to walk for some four or five miles, the road being all but impassable for horses. There is one most glorious prospect towards Scutari and Antivari; the track there makes a tremendous dip into a narrow ravine, and, on the left hand, at the commencement of the succeeding mountain, is the little village of S. George. Here I made acquaintance with the priest, and was introduced to his wife. Miserably poor they were; his income amounting—so far as the Church is concerned—to about thirty florins a-year: but, as he said, he would not change situations with any "pastor"—to use his own term—in Christendom. He told me that neither he nor any of the Montenegrin priests ever preached, except some of the more learned ones at Christmas and Easter. I counted his library: it consisted of eight volumes. His church was built in the seventeenth century: there is nothing whatever noticeable in it, though the iconostasis has somewhat better paintings than might be expected in such an out-of-the-way spot.

Thus we proceeded all day, with no further variation than the different degress of savageness of each succeeding ravine. But the water-shed of the mountains once passed, the scenery improved, and several of the glens were covered with bushes and low underwood, and then, as we penetrated more and more into the country, with really fine trees. The latter —now at the very end of May—were almost in full leaf; but here and there the snow lay in patches under them. At length, about 6 o'clock, we stood on the summit of the last mountain-range, and saw the long, narrow plain of Cettigne stretching at our feet.

The last information, so far as I know, which English travellers have received of the strange little principality (perhaps, at some distant time, to be the germ of a powerful kingdom), of which Cettigne is capital, is that which occurs in the very interesting travels of Sir Gardiner Wikinson. The reigning Vladika at that time, who, as had always been the case till then, united in himself the Royal and Metropolitical character, was Peter II.;—to give him his official title, "Metropolitan of Scanderia and the Sea Coast, Archbishop of Cettigne, Exarch of the Holy Throne of Pek, Vladika of Tchernagora, Peter II, Petrovitch Negush." In these amusing pages may be read the warlike feats of this prelate, his extraordinary skill with the rifle, and various details of his battles with the Turks. He was a man of gigantic size and strength, 6 feet 7 inches in height, and proportionately stout.

The principality of Montenegro being vested in its Metropolitans, it necessarily followed that descent from father to son was impossible: the eldest nephew succeeded the uncle. The above-named Vladika had thus succeeded his namesake, Peter I, who died in 1830, and who was venerated by his people as well for his great courage in war, as for his charity in peace. As soon as the new Metropolitan had been consecrated at St. Petersburg, he, of his own authority, and without consulting either the Holy Governing Synod or the Throne of Constantinople, forthwith canonised his uncle, and removed the body—as I shall have occasion hereafter to describe at length—into a chapel adjacent to the great church. This action was not viewed favourably at St. Petersburg; but explanations were given, and the Holy Synod at length professed itself satisfied. And certainly, no favourite saint ever had deeper veneration from the popular mind than has that S. Peter, with whom every Montenegrin, past middle life, was actually on familiar terms of intimacy.

Peter II, after having, by his prowess, secured himself from all danger on the part of the Turks, was endeavouring, in 1848, the year in which Sir Gardiner Wilkinson visited him, to mitigate the barbarous manner of Montenegrin warfare. To bring back so many heads of the Turks was then the great object of their guerilla expeditions.

But, notwithstanding the enormous strength and robust health of the Vladika, it appears that the seeds of a treacherous disease were in his constitution, even when he was in communication with Sir Gardiner; and shortly after the latter had left the country they developed rapidly. I have been told that it was a most touching thing to see him, knowing how much of his influence among his people depended on his personal strength and agility, endeavour to make efforts which were manifestly beyond his strength, till at length he was scarcely able to mount his horse; and, finally, was compelled to confine himself to his ecclesiastical duties. Utterly wasted away with decline, he died in 1850, leaving instructions that he should be buried at the very summit of Mount S. Nicholas, one of the loftiest of the Montenegrin range, in a chapel, for the erection of which, he left the funds from his private property. This little white chapel is a conspicuous object in every direction from the heights above Cattaro; and it seems to me that the original name is likely to be superseded by that of the Vladika Gora. He was succeeded by his nephew Daniel, then only just of age, and who, according to the tradition of the country, was bound to be consecrated Bishop as soon as he should attain to canonical years. But, feeling in himself no vocation for the Ecclesiastical state, he resolved, if it were possible, to break through the ancient *régime*. He first went to St. Petersburg, where he induced the Emperor to enter into his views; then to Paris, where he formed a very intimate friendship with Louis Napoleon, and received his assurance that France would interpose no obstacle to his wishes; and at the same time, Austria evinced the same favourable dispositions. Fortified by these external permissions, and finding that the Council of Montenegro had no strong feeling against the secularization of their principality, he went to Trieste, proposed to the daughter of one of the richest merchants of that city, obtained her hand, and settled himself in the Palace, of which more presently.

The city of Cettigne—if city such a collection of houses may be called—stands nearly in the centre of a somewhat ugly plain, perhaps six miles in length by two in breadth, through the turf of which the rock continually crops up. The whole place may be regarded as in the shape of a reversed $\mathbf{I}$; the inn forming the points of the termination of the letter; the lower line, which, however, is on the opposite side of the road, the houses of the few inhabitants which are usually occupied by the senators; the upper stroke, partly by stables or other erections of a similar kind, partly by one or two of the more respectable tenements; partly at the upper end, by the Palace and Monastery. Just before we arrived at the first houses, we observed a group of some three or four hundred persons drawn up in a circle round a speaker, who was haranguing them with great earnestness. It was, we were told, a council of war; and though I was unable to catch a single syllable that the Prince, who was the speaker, uttered, it was very easy to understand the formula of approbation,—"Be it as thou wilt, O Vladika!" with which the Assembly broke up. The Prince, who was in a most gorgeous uniform of gold and purple, walked first, followed by his commander-in-chief, who is also his brother-in-law, and some other of his state officers, towards the so-called Mall,—a marshy, unpleasant meadow which serves for military exercises. We sent our introductions to him, and in the meantime made perquisitions into the accommodation of the inn,—the most utterly filthy and vermin-haunted that, out of Portugal, I have ever beheld. In about a quarter of an hour we received a message, through the Commander-in-chief, to wait on the Prince. We found him in the Mall, at the upper end of a double line of his subjects, apparently of all ranks and conditions, engaged as the umpire of athletic contests. The ground between the two lines was measured out for flat leaps; and there were appliances near at hand for high leaps. The Prince himself had in his mouth an immense chibouque which rested on the ground; and the brilliancy of his dress contrasted remarkably with the half-clothed, ragged appearance of many of the bystanders and performers. Nothing could be more courteous than the Prince's behaviour while the gymnastic exercises were going on. After enquiring about our past route and future intentions, he expressed his sorrow that the Archbishop, on whom the Ecclesiastical government had now devolved, was absent on a pastoral visit in a distant part of his diocese,—Berda. He even offered, if we could wait two days, to summon him back again, in order that we might receive from him the most exact account of the ecclesiastical arrangement of the province. He then expressed his pleasure that a definitive line had been drawn by Commissioners, an English and French engineer, between the Montenegrin and Turkish possessions; so that, instead of being compelled, like his ancestors, to fix his capital in a place so inaccessible, so barren, so bleak as Cettigne, excluding all possibility of trade by the same obstacles which prevented the approach of the Turks, he should now be able to found a new city by the side of a navigable river, in a rich, fertile plain, and with the advantage of an Italian climate. The language in which he spoke was French, which he used fluently; while he seemed to speak Italian and German with the same ease. The future city he proposed to call from his own name, Danieloberg. I little thought, as I listened to him then, so full of life and strength, discussing, with the brightest anticipations, the future fortunes of his little State, that in a few months he would be lying in a bloody grave; and, in a few more, hostilities, on a more threatening scale than ever, would have burst out between his people and their perpetual oppressors.

We witnessed these exercises till dark; and the Prince was then kind enough to provide us with apartments by ejecting some of the senators; and with food, by sending it down from the Palace. That night was remarkable for one of the most tremendous thunderstorms that I ever remember; but at an early hour, we woke to find the morning bright and cloudless. Our first object was the Palace. It is a quadrangle of two low storeys, though the side facing the green has only a wall. You pass under a kind of oriel below the entrance porch, and the Prince's dwelling-house lies on your right hand. The rooms are but small, and rather overloaded with pictures. Among those in the reception-room are the Emperors and Empresses of Russia and France,—the latter, the peculiar friend and patron of Prince Daniel, who, indeed, received a pension from that Court. Here, after for so long a time having heard nothing but foreign languages, it was a pleasure to be introduced to an English lady, who was charged with the education of the Prince's little daughter,—his only child. From her we heard much of the unremitting exertions which the Prince has made in promoting education and civilisation. In fact, a single glance at the outbuildings of the Palace, as compared with the account of them given in Wilkinson's book, shows what an advance has been made: much of it, probably, owing to the fact of a lady's being at the head of the Court. Then, every battlement bristled with the head or skull of some unfortunate Turk; now, it had no other ornament than flowers. We heard bitter complaints of the severity of the winter, and the eager expectation with which an Italian January was looked forward to for the next—that is, the present—year. Hence we visited a billiard-room in the course of erection, and the garden; and, after this, the church. The latter forms a part of the original monastery, in which the Vladikas lived, while they were ecclesiastics; since that time, retaining only a few monks, it has been turned into a place of education. The church is Romanesque, and very small. It consists of apse, two little transepts, and nave. The apse-arch is plain First Pointed; the nave is two bays, also First Pointed. At the east end of the south transept lies the shrine of S. Peter: it is simply a bier with its hearse, over which a pall is thrown, there being no picture or other external symbol. The tower has a low, pyramidal head. The façade of the monastery has three stages. The upper is a series of circular arches, supported on short circular piers, with square base and square cap. The second, of the same arches with square shafts. The third, of obtuse arches of construction, rising not more than two feet from the ground. You enter the church at the right hand of this façade, by a kind of vestibule, additional to the south transept. Hence we went to the armoury, also contained in the monastery. It is the most singular collection of scymetars, guns, pistols, lances, horsetails, battered helmets and cuirasses—every possible fragment of wood and steel, which can give an idea of hand-to-hand engagements, from the time of the battle of Lepanto to this. They are heaped together without any attempt at arrangement,—pieces of the sixteenth century, with others captured only last year; the merest fragment, with the uninjured rifle of yesterday. On several of them one may notice a deep dark stain, that shows at the cost of how fierce a struggle they were obtained.

Having thus seen all that Cettigne has of interest, and the provinces beyond its second range of mountains asking a longer time to explore them than we had to give, it only remained for us to take a different course back to Cattaro. The Prince recommended that we should visit, on our way, the chapel in which the last Vladika is interred; and, accordingly, we started with that intention. The road was somewhat more savage than that of yesterday; but, after all, partly from the yet remaining snow, and partly from the effects of the thaw, we found it impossible to reach the pinnacle on which the little church is perched like an eagle. Striking back again, then, into our old course, after ten hours' riding, we saw beneath us the lovely Canal of Cattaro, the opposite mountains, the silver line of the Adriatic beyond them, the high fortifications to our left, and were welcomed down the many zigzags of the last descent by the cathedral bells chiming for vespers. Reaching our old quarters, we sent Dundich to the steamer just arrived from Corfu, to make arrangements for our return passage; and, at a little after ten that night, found ourselves, to our great content, very comfortably at our ease in one of the excellent berths of this large vessel.

Chapter XII.

RAGUSA; LESINA; HOME.

I Have no design of writing the very interesting history of Ragusa. Wilkinson and Paton have anticipated such a task. I have only, after reminding the reader that it never yielded to the dominion of Venice, to recount what it possesses in the way of ecclesiology. Its freedom from the Queen of the Adriatic is curiously recorded by the two slips of Turkish ground, which intersect the Austrian territory to the right and to the left of that which was the ancient republic. The road through these strips is neutral ground; the country on each side, even down by the sea, belongs to the Turk. That to the south, runs down by a place called Xvigne; that to the north, a little above Gravosa.

The steamers do not go into Ragusa, but into the bay of Gravosa, which lies on the northern side of the promontory on which the town itself stands. This, with its adjunct, the Val d'Ombla, is (with the exception of Cattaro) the most lovely scenery in Dalmatia. Wilkinson well says:—

"The entrance of the Val d'Ombla is a short way to the N.W. of Gravosa; and an hour's row brings you to the end of that picturesque valley. At the first village, on entering it, is a sulphureous spring, very similar to that of Spalato. Advancing up the estuary, or *loch*, the beauty of the scenery increases; and, as its course is winding, a diversity of views present themselves. The lower part of the hills is covered with a variety of foliage; amidst which the dark green of the cypress contrasts well with the grey olive, that thrives here, and bears much fruit; and rock and wood, hamlet and villa, mingled together and reflected in the water, with the circle of mountains above, form a succession of beautiful pictures; a principal feature of which is the Church of the Franciscan Convent, standing on a point of land near the end of the valley; where the river expands into the loch.*

This river is the ancient Ario or Arion."
A mile and a-half through a series of villas and their ruins: the suburbs of Ragusa having been entirely ruined by an expedition of the Montenegrins in 1805. In the times of their glory, when the word *argosy* spread the fame of the merchant republic to every sea, the principal men of the state had their country houses along the road we now pass; it commands a lovely view of the bay, with the islands of Daxa and Calamotta; and here, more luxuriantly than anywhere else in Dalmatia, the palm tree flourishes.

Ragusa, in Illyrian *Dubrovnik* (the wooded city,—from *Dubrava*, wood), in Turkish, *Paprovnik*—cannot be expected to offer much in the way of ecclesiology. It had already suffered from earthquakes in 1520, 1521, 1639; when on the 6th of April, 1667, a more

* The size of this sheet of water, and the short distance from which the river comes, before it expands into this great breadth, are alluded to in the verses of Elio Cervino:

"Danubio, et Nilo non vilior Ombla fuisset,
 Si modo progressus posset habere suos."

tremendous convulsion occurred, by which the city was almost destroyed. "It was only announced by the effects of the sudden shock itself, which destroyed every building except the fortresses, the lazaretto, and some edifices of solid construction. The sun had scarcely risen two hours; the inhabitants were mostly in their houses, or at prayers in the churches; and 5,000 individuals were in an instant buried beneath the ruins. The crash of falling walls, the rocking of the earth, the groans of the dying, and the tears of those who had escaped, presented a scene of horror and dismay. The ships in the port were dashed against each other, the sea rose to an unusual height, the wells were dried up, and a dense cloud of sand filled the air. No one felt secure; the dread of a second shock appalled the boldest; and fear only subsided to give place to grief, for the death or sufferings of relatives and friends. All had to lament the loss of some one who was dear to them; and the deaths of the Rettore Ghetaldi and other distinguished citizens were felt to be a public misfortune. Nine tenths of the clergy were killed; and a whole school of boys, who some days afterwards were heard to cry for water, beneath the fallen walls, perished miserably, without the means of rescue. Smaller shocks continued at intervals; many persons fled to Gravosa; and so great was the fear of approaching the ruins and tottering walls, that none thought of extinguishing the fires, that had been kindled among the fallen rafters of the houses and the public ovens. A strong wind springing up spread the flames in every direction; and no sooner had the fire ceased, than a band of Morlacchi, who had come to the market, began to pillage whatever the fire had spared; while the inhabitants, intent upon their own safety, or engaged in assisting their friends, were unable to interfere; and those who ventured to oppose them were murdered, for defending the property they had saved.

The Senate, in the meantime, neglected no duty of humanity required at such a moment; and every effort was made to check disorder, and repair the calamity. The gates were shut, to exclude other bands of Morlacchi, who were coming from the hills; and measures were immediately taken, to rescue the wounded from the ruins.

Confidence was at length restored; and the people, encouraged by the advice and consent of the nobles, having overcome the first impulse of fear, which had suggested the abandonment of their city, made every effort to rebuild their habitations. Four families only followed the example of the archbishop, who, with some monks, and numerous nuns, fled to Ancona." Earthquakes, more or less violent, are felt every twenty years; the last occurred on the 14th of September, 1843.

Passing through a pleasant faubourg, where, under a group of lofty trees, vehicles* ply for hire, we entered by a gate, the first which did not bear the Lion of S. Mark, but has instead the tutelar image of S. Biagio (S. Blaise) we put up at the Corona d'Ungheria.

Alas for the Cathedral! it would have been, but for

---

* A curious change since the time of Wilkinson, who says (vol. i. p. 372) " Ragusa has neither carriages, nor draught horses, everything being carried by porters."

the earthquake, of the greatest interest, having been founded by our Richard Cœur de Lion, on his return from the East. But it utterly perished; and the present Cathedral of S. Biagio is an Italian building, entirely worthless. The city was originally under the protection of SS. Sergius and Bacchus, to whom a Cathedral was erected by Paulimir, in 691; but the head of S. Blaise having been brought over from Armenia by a pilgrim priest in the tenth century, and that priest having been warned by the Prelate, in a dream, of an impending attack of the Venetians, the inhabitants, out of gratitude for their deliverance, assumed the Asiatic Bishop as their proper Saint. The architect was Angelo Bianchi; the building was finished in 1713. The sacristy contains a collection of inestimable value to the student of mediæval goldsmith's work. The reliquaries which hold the head of S. Biagio, procured as above-mentioned; his left arm, given by Venice, in 1346; his right arm, a present from Thomas Palæologus, despot of Peloponnesus, in 1459, seemed to me, as well as I could see in their dark recess, to display the most exquisite art. But there must be forty different pieces at least, brought hither for safety from imperilled monasteries in Bosnia and Herzegovina, of first-rate importance. I could have cried with vexation at being separated from so invaluable a treasure by only an iron screen; but no entreaties, no bribes, though I offered *twenty florins* to be allowed to see them but for one hour, could prevail on the sexton to open them. The Bishop himself, he said, could not give me permission without a capitular act. It was the only time the Imperial recommendation failed.

The Ragusan moonlight is celebrated all over Europe; and, certainly, as we came back late at night, from our first visit to the city, and saw the bay of Gravosa quivering under its sweet influence, and the white monastery of Val d'Ombla beyond the water, glimmering from its grove of pines and cypresses, I did think that nothing in the world could be so lovely.

It was on my second visit to Ragusa that I explored the Dominican Convent. The church itself is perfectly modernised—a mere oblong room—though with bits here and there, which shew it to have been, like the monastery, First-Pointed. The east end is square; the Chancel domed. There are a good many old fragments behind the High Altar: I copied from a small slab at the east end—

> Hic requiescit
> dn̄s Ursacius dicerevc
> cum suis heredibus
> Obiit MCCCXV.
> die primo Elmo.

the last line of which I cannot understand. I observed also an approximation to the usage of the Eastern Church, in the number of crowned pictures suspended round the walls of the building.

The cloisters are far more interesting. They form a tolerable sized quadrangle, of five bays each way. They are First-Pointed; each division contains three arches; the shafts are circular with square Corinthianising cap, and circular, on square, base. Between each two, above a small quatrefoil, is a very elegant ornament of three intersecting triangles.

I have called this work First-Pointed. Yet from

its identity with other work in this same city, which we know to be of Third-Pointed date, from a certain leanness and baldness of its mouldings, and from a refinement very unlike the rude honesty of the undoubtedly First-Pointed work at Curzola and in other of the islands, I am almost inclined to think that this is in truth Ragusan Third-Pointed, giving way to one of the tricks, not unusually played by that style; and on which Mr. Webb has some excellent remarks, in his Continental Ecclesiology, page 376. I am the more inclined to believe this, from the arcading of several of the shops which surround the Cathedral; and which bear no token whatever of the remote antiquity which they would at first seem to promise.

In the monastery we were received, as usual, with great courtesy; and though the greater part of the library was sold by the monks at the French invasion, there remain about fifty manuscripts of considerable value; and I spent several hours in copying sequences from them. Hence we visited the Franciscan Monastery which, except for the library, has little of interest. The quadrangle, though very much mutilated, is at least pretty with its variety of semi-tropical plants, which trail over its walls. The church itself is entirely modern: its tower is lofty, of four stages, its upper ones with baluster windows, and the whole surmounted by an octagonal cupola. In a somewhat elaborate Flamboyant south door, the tympanum has a well carved *Mater Dolorosa*.

I had a great desire to visit the first Turkish village, Bertano, only three miles from hence. My companion preferred to explore, at leisure, the treasures of the

Dominican convent. I went, therefore, with Dundich, to the Boschetto, a pleasant little grove just outside of the southern gate—this gate, by the way, like all the others, is flanked by square mediæval turrets, and possesses no real strength;—and from the bazaar there, we hired two miserably lean horses, and were informed that no passport was necessary. The road immediately began to ascend, curving round the gulf of Brenno, just by a place called Porte Plocce, and then by zigzags ascending the hill. Behind us lay the old city girt in by its curious mediæval fortifications; beyond it, the lovely Val d'Ombla; to the immediate right, the gulf of Brenno, with the little island, sometimes called Croma, sometimes S. Marco. On this latter, the Archduke Maximilian has laid out, we were told, 30,000 florins, partly on a fortification, partly on a Franciscan house. Across the bay, lay the decayed village of Ragusa Vecchia, the ancient Epidaurus; beyond this, fenced in by high cliffs on either side, and stretching towards Cattaro, the valley Ville Ligna; and to the north of the latter, snow-capped Mount Sniegsizza. As soon as we had surmounted the highest zigzag, Bertano lay immediately on the opposite side of the glen; and the first minaret that I ever saw, was at that very moment capped with a horribly black thunder cloud—no bad emblem of a race sitting in darkness, and the shadow of death. The village itself was as wretched and filthy as most of those in Herzegovina, though nearly a moiety of the inhabitants are, I believe, Greeks. Neither in the orthodox Church, nor in the Mosque, is there anything of the slightest interest.

We returned to Gravosa through a second lovely evening. The nightingales were singing from every bush by the wayside; and the mixture of these with fireflies, palm-trees, hoopoos, and the aloe, seemed to us a strange yet beautiful confusion of England and the tropics. At Gravosa, we hired a boat, and crossing to Val d'Ombla, visited the neat little Dominican convent there. It has nothing in the way of architecture to interest the traveller, any more than the smaller house of the Jesuits, on the opposite side of the bay. But I never saw anything more lovely, as we walked the quarter-deck late at night, than the gradual rising of the moon over the mountains, the darkening shade of the cypress groves, and the beautiful reflection of the white convent in the unruffled lake.

At 8 o'clock the next morning, having in the night coasted the outside of Meleda, and run between Curzola and Lagosta, we found ourselves rapidly passing Lesina, the ancient Pharos, by a corruption of which name it is called, in Slavonic, Hvar. In primitive writers it has won the title of Sancta, on account of the great number of its martyrs. It may be forty-two miles in length, while it varies in breadth from two miles to seven and a-half. We cast anchor off the town of Lesina, at the western extremity of its island, at 8 A. M. A very picturesque place it is, with its Venetian lines of architecture, and the rich creamy yellow colour of its houses. In its steep steppy streets, and their excessive narrowness, it reminded me strongly of Curzola.

Santo Spirito was the first church; a very small, rude, Romanesque building.

<small>Lesina
S. Spirito.</small>

The apse is circular, the nave of three bays, the roof very acutely pointed, and clearly later. There is a miraculous image of S. Mary, which has acquired considerable celebrity. The west door is square-headed, under a pointed arch of construction. The shafts of the doorway are voluted, with heads at the upper angles. In the tympanum is an ancient figure, under a trefoiled arch; and in the apex of the western façade, a ten-leaved rose, each leaf trefoiled.

<small>Cathedral.</small>

Higher up the hill is the *Cathedral*, —a building sadly modernized, yet not without its interest. The choir seems divided into two portions, the eastern quite modern, the western in three bays, like Santo Spirito. The floor is of red and white marble. The seven stalls on each side with subsellæ are much admired by the natives: they are fair Flamboyant work. The ambones are more remarkable. Each is octagonal, supported on four shafts; the shafts themselves circular, with octagonal flowered capitals, and circular, on square, bases. They are still used and vested. Besides these, there is, at the entrance of the choir, a stone desk, supported by a circular shaft, which proceeds from the back of a lion,—the whole a very singular composition. The nave, which is modernized, has four bays: the pictures which ornament it, have the Greek type very strongly. West of the south aisle are some singular frescoes: highest of all, the Madonna; under that, S. Catherine and S. Lucy; under these, two figures with a lamb and a book, and another with an open book; under these, the Twelve Apostles. The tower, to the west of the north aisle, has five stages; the upper pierced with four, the next with three, the next with two, and the next with one, circular light. Not far from this, near the centre of the Quay, are the *Loggie*, built by San Michaeli, and bearing S. Mark's lion. Near to this is the Venetian tower of S. Mark, the church of which was destroyed by lightning some years ago.

This is the last church with which the reader will be troubled.

On leaving Lesina, we immediately passed the island of Lissa, celebrated from the victory obtained by Captain Hoste, over a French squadron, and which I cannot describe better than in Mr. Paton's words:—

" This French force consisted of four frigates of 44 guns, two corvettes of 32 guns, and three sloops, with 700 infantry on board. That of Captain Hoste, off Lesina, consisted of the 'Amphion,' 32; the 'Active,' 38; the 'Cerberus,' 32; and 'Volage,' of 22; or 880 Britons to 2,500 French and Italians. What's in a name? Wonders. With such appalling odds against him, the gallant Hoste felt that something was necessary to produce a moral effect in so critical a moment; and the telegraphic word, 'Remember Nelson!' thrilled through every heart, while prolonged cheers echoed from deck to deck of the little squadron.

" Close to the eastern shore of Lissa, the 'Amphion,' Captain Hoste, with the 'Active,' 'Volage,' and 'Cerberus,' in close order, awaited the enemy, who bore down from the north-east. Dubourdieu, in the

'Favorite,' led the van; and marking the 'Amphion,' which lay next the shore, for his own, he prepared to board her, while his other frigates and small craft might make easy work of the 'Active,' the 'Volage,' and the 'Cerberus.' A crowd of seamen and marines thronged the forecastle of the French vessel ('Favorite.') Dubourdieu himself stood forward to direct and encourage his men; and so close was the 'Favorite' to the 'Amphion,' that eager expectation could be read on the countenances of the men. The grappling tackle was ready, the cutlass was drawn, and the pike was prepared; but just when a few yards separated the two ships, off went a five-and-a-half-inch howitzer with 750 musket-balls from the quarter-deck of the 'Amphion;' and as if Death in his own person had swept his scythe from gunwale to gunwale, Dubourdieu and his boarders were prostrate in an instant. Foiled in the attempt, the Captain of the French frigate, who now took the command, attempted to pass round between the 'Amphion' and the shore, and thus place Hoste between two fires; but so nicely and narrowly had the 'Amphion' chosen her position, that the 'Favorite' got ashore in the attempt, and was thus in a great measure *hors de combat*. This important incident gave such a turn to the struggle as the French never recovered; but the odds being still against the English, the contest was prolonged for several hours. The British squadron now stood on the larboard tack; but the 'Cerberus,' in wearing, got her rudder choked by a shot, which caused a delay; but the action continued. Captain Hoste, in the 'Amphion,' being now galled by the fire of the 'Flore,' 44, and the 'Bellona,'

32, closed with the former, and in a few minutes the
'Flore' struck; but having received by mistake some
shots of the 'Bellona,' which were intended for and
went past the 'Amphion' after she had struck, an
officer took her ensign, and, holding it over the taffrel,
threw it into the sea. Hoste now crossed to the
'Bellona,' and compelled her also to strike at noon,
just three hours after the action began; but no sooner
was this accomplished, than the 'Flore,' belying her
surrender, was seen crowding sail to escape, pursuit
by the 'Amphion' being by this time impossible, her
foremast threatening to fall, and her sails and rigging
rendered unserviceable from the cross-fires she had
sustained. The rest of the Gallo-Venetian squadron,
upon this, attempted to escape; but the British
'Active,' pursuing the Venetian 'Corona,' compelled
her also to strike, in a running fight, at half-past 2 in
the afternoon; thus terminating one of the most
gallant actions on record. Three 44-gun frigates, including the escaped 'Flore,' and a 32-gun corvette
having struck to the British squadron.

"Lissa thenceforth became to the end of the war
an English possession. Colonel Robertson was civil
and military Governor. Twelve natives formed a legislative and judicial council. A small fort was constructed, and the towers to this day bear the names of
Wellington, Bentinck, and Robertson."

Thirty-six hours after leaving Lesina, we came
once more in sight of the southernmost promontory of
Istria. It was a calm, lovely summer night; a glossy,
leaden hue on the still waters. As I walked the
quarter-deck during its earlier hours, first I made out

the bay-entrance of the harbour of Pola; then I caught the Compline or, probably, Matin, bell from Santa Catherina; then light behind light, at Grongera, at Rovigno, at Parenzo, flashed along the darkening shore. There I bade farewell to beautiful Istria; and once more, at 7 o'clock the next morning, we found ourselves at the quay of Trieste.

That night—a night of storm and rain—we crossed the Adriatic, and had our first view of its Queen on Whitsunday morning. Hence, giving a few days to that glorious city and to Milan, we arrived at Turin. And so, over Mont Cenis, to S. Jean de Maurienne. Here I would recommend the little Cathedral, still curious, though modernized, and its singular Sacraments-house, to the traveller with a vacant hour. Here, also, I heard the bitter complaint of the inhabitants at their proposed transference to France,—a transference to take place in the week immediately succeeding that of my visit.

Thus, by Chambery and Macon, to Paris; and our old route viâ Calais and Dover, closed a very happy, and (to me at least) instructive, tour.

THE END.

INDEX.

	Page
S. Agatha	17
S. Antonio (Veglia)	93
Aquileia Cathedral	46
Aussee, Church	19
Chapel	20
Baura	8
Begliano	44
Besca Nuova	105
Besca Valle	104
Bruck, Minorites	26
Buje Cathedral	73
Capo d'Istria, Cathedral	67
Capuchins	68
Observantines	69
Cattaro, Cathedral	165
S. Luke	168
S. Spiridion	169
S. Catherine (Island)	83
Cettigne, Monastery ...	
Church	191
Curzola	
All Saints	160
Cathedral	159
S. Michael	159
Duino	42
S. Fosca	96
Geishorn	24
S. George (Montenegro)	184
Gmunden	14
Goisling	17
Gratz	
Barmherzige Brüder	33
Cathedral	28

	Page
Gratz Ferdinandi-capelle	30
Franciscan	32
Mariä Himmel-fahrt	32
Pfarrkirche	31
Ursuliner-kirche	33
Hasbruch	4
S. Jean de Maurienne Cathedral	206
Lauffen	16
Leoben S. Maria	25
Lésina, Cathedral	202
S. Spirito	202
Lielzen	23
Linz Cathedral	7
Lussinpiccolo Cathedral	109
Macarska Concathedral....	158
Malinski	93
Marburg, Dom	35
S. Maria	72
Michelsdorff	26
Mitterndorff	23
Monfalcone	44
Parenzo Cathedral	79
Passau, Cathedral	5
S. Gertrude	6
Jesuits	5
Maria Hilf	6
S. Michael	5
S. Paul	5
Pirano, Cathedral	70
Franciscans	71
Madonna delle Salute	72
S. Pietro....	71
S. Stephano	72

	Page
Poglizza....	95
Pola, Cathedral....	86
Franciscans	88
Prosecco	41
Ragusa, Cathedral	197
Dominicans	198
Franciscans	199
Roitham	11
Rottenmann	24
Santpor	4
Sebenico, Cathedral	130
Dominican	133
Franciscan	133
S. Lucia	133
Madonna di Borgo	133
S. Maria Valle Verde	132
S. Pasquale	133
Selve (Island)	111
Spalato, Cathedral	149
S. Chiara	153
S. Giovanni Bapt.	151
S. Pasquale	153
Trieste Cathedral	38
Val d'Ombla	200
Veglia, Cathedral	98
Clarissines	101
S. Francisco	99
S. Maria	100
Visinada	74
Wilshofen	3
Zara, Cathedral....	116
S. Elias	122
S. Grisogono	121
S. Maria	120
S. Simeon	124
Zlatinski (in Bua)	156
Zoccolante	101

ERRATA.

Page 7, line 18.—*For* "to," *read* "her."
  ,, 14 ,, 9.—*For* "1446," *read* "1445."
  ,, 44 ,, 9.—*For* "Sanctorius," *read* "Sanctorum."
  ,, 78.—In the *engraving* of the tabernacle, read "Eufrasius" for "Fufrasius."
  ,, 102 ,, 22.—*Before* "One of them," *insert* "nevertheless."
  ,, 137 ,, 5.—*For* "Traugurium," *read* "Trau, the ancient Tragurium."
  ,, 158 ,, 27.—*For* "only," *read* "hardly."
  ,, 162 ,, 24.—The quotation from Penrose should end at "*geographical miles.*"
  ,, 165, last line.—*For* "de," *read* "die."
  ,, 173 line 1.—*For* "will be described hereafter," *read* "have been already described." It was at first intended that Chap. X should precede Chap. VIII.

www.ingramcontent.com/pod-product-compliance
Lightning Source LLC
Chambersburg PA
CBHW031815230426
43669CB00009B/1150